The
Everychurch
Guide to Growth

Growth

The Everychurch Guide to Growth

HOW ANY PLATEAUED CHURCH CAN GROW

Elmer Towns, C. Peter Wagner & Thom S. Rainer

BROADMAN
& HOLMAN
PUBLISHERS

Nashville, Tennessee

0–8054–0192–X

Published by Broadman & Holman Publishers, Nashville, Tennessee
Page Design and Typography: TF Designs, Mt. Juliet, Tennessee

Dewey Decimal Classification: 254
Subject Heading: CHURCH GROWTH
Library of Congress Card Catalog Number: 98–16473

Library of Congress Cataloging-in-Publication Data
Towns, Elmer L.
The everychurch guide to growth / by Elmer Towns, C. Peter Wagner,
Thom S. Rainer
    p. cm.
    Includes bibliographical references.
    ISBN 0–8054–0192–X
    1. Church growth.   I. Wagner, C. Peter.   II. Rainer, Thom S.
III. Title.
BV652.25.T685 1998
254'.5—dc21
                                                                    98–16473
                                                                    CIP

1 2 3 4 5 02 01 00 99 98

Contents

Foreword

I was asked to write the Foreword to this book for two reasons. I have pastored churches in all three categories: a small church in Hillham, Indiana, with only three people in my first service; second, Faith Memorial Church in Lancaster, Ohio, with approximately 500 people when I became pastor in 1974; and Skyline Wesleyan Church, Greater San Diego, California, with 1,000 in attendance when I became pastor in 1981. All three of these churches broke the barrier in front of them, so I agree with what has been written and praise God for this book. I pray God will use it to help other churches break barriers facing them.

The second reason I was asked to write the Foreword is because the organization I founded, Injoy, sponsors two different seminars to break barriers. C. Peter Wagner conducts a seminar called "Breaking the 200 Barrier." I consider C. Peter Wagner the premier church growth authority, a leader with insight into the causes that keep churches from growing. Next, Elmer Towns is the keynote speaker for the Injoy-sponsored conference entitled "Breaking the 1,000 Barrier." Although ten additional speakers participate in this conference by offering testimonies of how they broke the 1,000 barrier, Elmer Towns has been my personal mentor. He was the first national leader who came to my church in

Lancaster, Ohio, to guide me as Faith Memorial Church broke the 1,000 barrier.

Thom S. Rainer is a new friend, and I love him because he loves growing churches. He loves small churches, middle-sized churches, and large churches; and he loves to do research on church growth. I am intrigued by his insights on the causes of growth.

Each of these three writers brings unique strength to the book. As I read their contributions, I saw their personalities shine through their writings. Peter is a warm scholar who loves people and churches, and Peter's love for the church is clearly reflected in his section. He does not put a guilt trip on pastors of small churches that cannot grow. Rather, Peter has told them that it is all right in certain situations not to grow. Sometimes a person can have a tremendous pastoral ministry where growth is impossible. However, Peter also offers the right strategy and plans for the small church that wants to and can grow.

Thom S. Rainer is the dean of the Billy Graham School of Evangelism, Church Growth and Missions at The Southern Baptist Theological Seminary in Louisville, Kentucky. To be a dean one must be scholarly, research oriented, and given to great detail. However, a seminary dean must also be an experienced pastor if he is going to effectively train young seminarians to pastor churches. Thom Rainer qualifies as that scholarly researcher with pastoral experience. As I read his section, I examined the research he did and loved his chapters.

Elmer Towns brings a historical quality to church growth. Peter Wagner says that Elmer Towns's book, *The Ten Largest Sunday Schools*, was the first American church growth book. When I pastored a little church in Hillham, Indiana, Towns's book on the largest Sunday Schools set my heart afire. It made me want to build a large church and to reach thousands of people. God used that book to put within my heart a desire to be all I could be. I knew I could pastor a large church. Towns is the pioneer in the field of church growth. He knows the megachurch movement in

America from the beginning. He knows the megachurch movement from the inside out, because he went to work for one of the largest churches in America, Thomas Road Baptist Church in Lynchburg, Virginia. He cofounded a college in that church, Liberty University. Towns teaches a Sunday School class with more than one thousand people in a megachurch. This experience qualifies him to know experientially the megachurch's problems, strengths, passion, and reason for existence. I know of no person who is more qualified and gifted to write a chapter on the megachurch than Elmer Towns.

If you love the church of Jesus Christ, you'll love this book. It is a labor of love by three friends who love each other, who love the work of the church, and who love the author of the church, Jesus Christ.

My prayer is that God would use this book to motivate many to grow churches in America. I am interested in every aspect of growth, both internal and external. We must always remember that growth begins by winning people to Jesus Christ, people who otherwise would go to hell. Then they are added to the church and involved in the life and service of the church. Then they are built up in Christ and become mature in Christ. I am interested in influencing culture and changing lives to bring honor to the Lord Jesus Christ. I am interested in bringing added glory to the God we serve.

Everyone who knows Injoy and my ministry knows I have made a commitment to equip ten thousand pastors to build a super church, and I have a goal to enlist one million prayer partners to pray for their pastors. While these are only a few of my goals, they directly relate to this manuscript. I pray that God would use this book together, with my ministry, to quickly build ten thousand megachurches in the United States.

What about the small church and the medium-sized church? I am asking God to give us one million laypeople who will pray for their pastors and churches. When this happens, all churches will become spiritually healthy and will grow to bring glory to the Lord Jesus Christ.

May God accomplish the purposes for which the authors of this book have written. May God cause the churches of the world to grow, and may God bring glory to himself through these pages.

Sincerely,
John C. Maxwell, Founder
INJOY

Overcoming Barriers
Facing Growing
Churches

Whatever is alive will grow. And anytime growth takes place, barriers to growth will be present. Just as weeds will stop growth in a garden and germs or disease will hinder growth in the human body, so barriers can stop churches from growing. Growth and barriers go together like a sock on a foot; they must be studied together for understanding the growing church.

Growth is the most dynamic thing in life. Life is a gift of God to the farmer who grows crops. Life is the gift of God to parents who raise a baby, and life is a gift to pastors who lead a church. Growth means life . . . energy . . . new horizons . . . new freedoms . . . new attainments. Growth means the fulfillment of expectations.

Barriers to Babies

A growing baby must overcome three obstacles. First, a baby in the arms of his mother is laid on the floor, immobile. The first problem is motion; the baby must learn to roll over or crawl. When the baby learns to crawl, he or she has overcome the first barrier of motion. Now the baby has freedom to go where he or she chooses, however, not very far. Crawling is slow and tedious, and even though crawling gives freedom, it gives limited freedom.

The second obstacle is overcome when the child stands, releases the grip on a parent, and takes the first step. Walking gives the child a new, previously inexperienced freedom. The walking baby travels much faster than the crawling baby. Walking allows the baby the freedom of the room, the house, the yard, and ultimately the neighborhood.

The third barrier is communication. The baby is locked up in his own world of needs and desires. A baby can only communicate by crying or showing other forms of displeasure. But through the interactive transmission of hearing and speaking, the child slowly learns to communicate with the outside world. The child slowly learns to intelligently ask a question or understand a response. The ability to talk overcomes another basic barrier to growth.

Church Growth Barriers

Three basic barriers face a church growing from infancy to the superchurch. While each of the barriers has many and varied reasons, these barriers are found at the upper-limits of the small church, the medium-sized church, and the large church. The first barrier is moving from a small church to a medium-sized church. The barrier seems to come at the point of approximately 100 in attendance. While some babies crawl at an earlier age than others, some churches face the small church barrier much earlier, that is, when they reach attendance of 50 or 60. Other churches reach this barrier much later, that is, when they reach attendance of 150 to 200.

Overcoming Church Growth Barriers
Small Church Barriers of 200 People
Middle Church Barriers of 400 People
Large Church Barriers of 1,000 People

There is no magical number to the first barrier; nor is there just one reason that keeps a church from growing. Understanding the multiple growth barriers and some of the tools to overcome the barriers will give direction to a pastor to help a church through this *window* growth season.

When the church reaches the medium size, an entirely new world of dynamics confronts its ministry and growth. Some medium-sized churches face a barrier when attendance reaches 250–350. Still, other middle-sized churches continue numerical growth; but because they still have all of the middle-sized characteristics, they face a barrier when attendance reaches 750.

A walking baby may get what he wants from anywhere in the room, or even walk anywhere in the house. But unless the child solves the next barrier facing his growth, he is locked into the world of infancy. So the medium-sized church must continue growing to move into the world of the large church.

Needs

Many pastors desire to break the 100 barrier, but that goal seems to be illusive . . . mystical . . . forbidding. They usually cross the 100 barrier first on a "high day," when the church has an event such as "Friend Day," "Anniversary Day," or a big attendance on Easter or Christmas. Once the 100 barrier is mentally broken the first time on a special day, it is easier to repeatedly break the barrier. Even then, however, it is usually some time before the church averages over 100 in attendance.

The next attendance barriers are either 200, 300, 400, or 500. The same process is followed in breaking these barriers. First the barrier is broken on special days, like Easter or a high attendance day. Eventually the church becomes a medium-sized church and begins to operate as a medium-sized church.

The same pattern is followed when a church breaks the 1,000 barrier. Once this happens, the church moves into entirely different infrastructures and leadership roles.

Reading this book will not guarantee you that your church will grow. Neither will an understanding of growth barriers give you the ability to break growth barriers, just like going through a class on evangelism will not make you a soul-winner. Many students attend classes on church growth and understand growth barriers and the principles by which barriers are broken. But knowledge is never the final key to growth, even though knowledge is the basis for that attainment.

The process of breaking growth barriers begins when you know why churches grow and what it takes to grow a church. The barrier begins to fall when you make a commitment to grow and start to act. To grow a church, you must have *leadership skills* to lead people through the tensions that come when you face barriers. Being a good leader presupposes you have *ministry skills* to help fill people's spiritual needs and cause them to grow as attendance grows. Because people are uneasy with change, you must have *relationship skills* to keep the people with you through barriers. Finally, you must have *management skills*, because as you grow, you will minister through committees and staff members. You will need to convince many people to take a trip with you as barriers that keep the church from growth are broken.

Certain individuals are "initiators"; winning is a way of life for them. They win at preaching and soul-winning, and they will grow a church to remain a "winner." When they know how to grow a church, they will pay the price to grow through barriers. They are described as aggressive individuals.

Skills Needed to Cross Growth Barriers	
1.	Leadership Skills
2.	Ministry Skills
3.	Relationship Skills
4.	Management Skills

This book is written for "initiators" and "winners." It will give them insight, ideas, and programs to grow a church. It will make breaking the barriers easier for them.

This book is not written to discourage anyone. Some pastors are "growers," even though they do not have aggressive personalities. They win but let "winning" come to them. They will let their church grow, but they will not set a goal to grow. They will let growth happen. They will minister to people, counsel people through their problems, and preach the Word of God. This book will help them by changing their perception of their roles and how they do ministry. Reading a book can't change a person's nature; a more passive person will not become aggressive. But any pastor can break the 1,000 barrier by letting it happen naturally.

Three Foundations to Break Barriers

While this book focuses on ideas, methods, and principles of breaking growth barriers, three foundational elements are needed to cause a church to grow. A growing pastor will lead a church to grow. The pastor will take the journey, and the members will go with him.

First, to build a church through growth barriers, take advantage of all the spiritual dynamics available to all believers. Learn brokenness before the Lord so God can fill you with his Spirit. Know the Word of God; it gives you authority in ministry. Be a person

---

Great Leaders Build Great Churches,

Average Leaders Build Average Churches,

Anti-Leaders Harm Churches.

---

of intercessory prayer. Minister from the calling you have from God. This calling will drive you to sacrifice, take up your cross daily, and follow Jesus Christ.

Years ago someone said, "The church is the length and shadow of its pastor." Therefore, you will grow a church out of your character and spirituality. A pastor will grow the type of church that reflects his personal growth, not what he writes in a vision or ministry statement.

Spiritual Pastors Build Spiritual Churches,

Praying Pastors Build Praying Churches,

Soul-Winning Pastors Build Evangelistic Churches,

---

and

Aggressive Pastors Build Aggressive Churches.

While some pastors build successful churches, they are the type of people who would build a successful hamburger stand, a big contracting business, or would be successful in any area of life. These kind of people will use business principles to grow a church, but we need to ask, "Is it a spiritual church in God's sight?" Also, "Is it a New Testament church?"

Therefore, you must be godly to build a church of God. The law of the embryonic seed determines the type of church that grows. The kind of seed sown in the ground determines the quality of the fruit that grows on the stalk.

Second, a pastor must get out of his own way to grow a church. Some pastors cannot reach 1,000 because they continually sabotage themselves. They have misconceptions about growth, misconceptions about causes of growth, misconceptions about ministry, and misconceptions about the principles of God that give life and cause growth.

Some pastors who were growing a church twenty-five years ago have gotten in their way through legalism. They feel that separation from sin is the way to build a church, so they emphasize separation. Thus, fewer unchurched people attend their services. The fewer unsaved to whom they can present Christ, the fewer people they have being converted. And the fewer they have converted, the less church growth is possible. While we believe in both sanctification and separation, we also know the preaching calendar must be balanced. Those who work around the nursery in the church realize they will have to deal with dirty diapers and toys spread all over the place. Babies will spill their milk and throw strained bananas on the floor. A church that doesn't go after the unchurched probably won't get babies in Christ, and that church won't have anyone to grow into spiritual maturity or who can separate from sin.

Third, some pastors refuse to develop leadership skills. They think their only roles are to preach and teach. A leaderless church can't grow. The pastor who refuses to develop leadership skills is like the golfer who ties one hand behind him and attempts to play golf.

It takes two wings to fly, two legs to walk, and two rails to allow a train to run. So it takes two influences to build a church. The first influence is ministry that builds up the individual to spiritual maturity. The second is leadership that influences the church organization to grow in numbers.

The pastor must be the minister to people and also the leader of people.

Three Foundations for Growth	
1.	The pastor must be growing to produce a growing church.
2.	The pastor must get out of his own way to grow a church.
3.	The pastor must develop leadership skills to grow a church.

Barriers That Hinder Growth

Barriers obviously keep some churches stuck in the small, middle, or large church grouping. These unique barriers will be addressed in the following chapters. At this point an overview of the principles of barriers taught by church growth leaders will be offered.

Why is it that some churches just don't grow? Part of the answer to that question is found in recognizing the barriers to evangelism. According to Donald McGavran, people like to become Christians without crossing racial, linguistic, or class barriers.

McGavran's statement is not a normative statement but rather a descriptive statement. This is not the way it should be; rather, it is the way it is. God made humans social creatures, and barriers that interfere with social relationships may have a profound spiritual influence on humans. The more barriers placed between a person and Christ, the more difficult it is to win him to Christ. If our churches are going to grow, we need to remove as many barriers as possible to make it easier for people to become Christians.

Of course some barriers can never be removed, barriers such as the offense of the cross. Some will never be saved because the message of the cross, which is an intricate part of the gospel, is offensive to them. Grace is also a barrier to some, for they want to do good works to be saved and resist being saved by grace alone (Eph. 2:8–9). We cannot remove these primary barriers. The

Barriers	
E-0	Internal Barriers
E-1	Stained-Glass Barriers
E-2	Cultural and Class Barriers
E-3	Language Barriers

barriers we can remove are secondary and are not directly related to the root of Christianity.

The E-1 barrier has been called *the stained-glass barrier*. Church growth writers speak of E-1 Evangelism, that is, evangelism that overcomes the church-building barrier. "Stained glass" reflects more than windows or church sanctuaries. It is symbolic of the things that prevent those outside the church from getting inside to hear the gospel. These barriers make it difficult for a person to attend Sunday School or a church service or continue to attend church. The stained-glass barrier includes such things as poor location, inadequate parking, and unkempt or poorly maintained facilities.

A full parking lot is a barrier for the visitor who must find a parking place in the street. However, some think that adequate parking or the elimination of other barriers will cause church growth. No! The church must have a dynamic that draws people to Jesus Christ. The church must have warm services, and the pastor must preach with power. A barrier just makes it harder to reach people; it does not make it impossible to reach people. Eliminating barriers makes it easier to reach people.

Stained-glass barriers also include perceptions, such as a lost person's dislike for a denomination's name or what an unchurched person remembers about a particular church. Some have had a bad experience with a church member from a certain denomination; hence the church name is a barrier. A church split can be a barrier to the neighborhood, making it harder for both halves to reach people for Christ.

The E-2 barrier is a *cultural and class barrier*. It hinders the evangelistic outreach of some churches. This principle recognizes members of certain cultures who may not wish to attend a church that predominantly consists of members of another culture. It is not a matter of liking the people of another culture or class; it is a matter of being comfortable with their different values. While the church must be the church of the open door, willing to admit all, members of a culture different from the members of the church will usually have difficulty becoming assimilated into the social life of the congregation.

The E-3 barrier is the barrier of overcoming distant cultures, such as Americans evangelizing Chinese. Perhaps the most obvious E-3 barrier to evangelism is language. People like to hear God in their heart language (the language in which they think), even when they also speak a second language.

A Sick Body Will Not Grow

The church must be healthy in order to grow. The best biblical analogy to represent the church is the body, and a physical body will grow when it is healthy, fed, and exercised. A body does not need to be challenged, coaxed, or have a goal to grow. The body automatically grows when it is healthy. When a local church body is healthy, it will grow internally and externally. If your church is not growing, you need to ask the questions: Are you properly feeding it the Word of God? Are you properly exercising your church in prayer and witnessing? If you think your church is healthy, but it is not growing, perhaps it has a disease. When the body has a disease, it does not grow in a healthy manner.

In medical school, pathology is one of the first courses studied by future doctors.[1] Pathology is the study of disease. A doctor cannot treat a sickness until he understands its causes. He must know what makes a person sick before he can suggest a remedy or prescription. Even then the doctor does not make a person well; the body has the energy to heal itself and grow itself. So it is with the body of Christ. When a church is sick, no leader can make it well. When he removes the cause of the illness, the body heals itself.

The following sections examine the diseases that prohibit a church from growing. When we know and remove the causes of church diseases, the body will heal itself.

Ethnikitis

The first disease is called "ethnikitis." It is the inbred allegiance of the church to one ethnic group and its lack of adaptation or openness to other groups. This disease occurs when communities change their ethnic character and churches fail to adapt to those changes. Sometimes a symptom of ethnikitis is what has been called "white flight," where the traditional WASP (White Anglo-Saxon Protestant) churches move out of their traditional communities as the ethnic character of the area changes.

In our growing nation, our churches must be multiethnic, reaching to every new family or group of people moving into our neighborhoods. In one sense, the small neighborhood church is a homogeneous unit, yet the growing church must be a heterogeneous unit (the open door to all people) made up of homogeneous cells (classes and cells that will attract and minister to each group within its neighborhood).

	How to Solve Ethnikitis
1.	Begin Bible classes or cells for new groups.
2.	Hire staff members who represent the new groups moving into the neighborhood.
3.	Begin a second-language preaching service.

4.	If the church moves to another neighborhood, dedicate the building to spawn a continuing church.
5.	Aggressively seek to bring new groups into the church. New groups do not automatically visit existing churches; they must be aggressively sought and brought into the church fellowship.

The church that suffers ethnikitis is first, sinning against God, second, disobeying the Great Commission, and third, allowing a cancer to fester within its body.

Ghost Town Disease

Ghost Town disease used to be called old age, another pathology of church growth. This disease describes the community more than the church. When a church and community become "old" so that not many people are moving in or out of the neighborhood, it is described as suffering from "old age." Though a stable community has many advantages, it also has some disadvantages. When no one is moving in, prospects for evangelism diminish, because the unchurched candidates for church membership decrease in number; hence no numerical growth can take place.

	How to Overcome Old Age
1.	Reach people going through transitions (the seasons of the soul) in the hospital ministry, weddings, funerals, birth of a baby, etc.
2.	Don't set unrealistic growth goals.
3.	Give attention to maintenance ministry, not growth ministry.
4.	Begin pioneer works in another community that is growing.

It is difficult to build a growing church in a stagnant neighborhood. When people are stable and not moving geographically, they are also probably not moving spiritually. And when people move out of a neighborhood (such as a dying mining town or a small farming town), it is difficult to see growth.

People-Blindness

A third disease of the church that can hinder growth is called "people-blindness." This refers to the inability of the church to see spiritual, social, and community needs. The key to an effective, growing ministry may be summarized in the expression "find a hurt and heal it." Hence, a church must have a "vision" of needs, then develop a program to meet the needs of its people and the community. A church with a food service for the poor will attract and minister to the poor. Some churches have ministries for the hearing impaired (sign language interpreting), classes for the mentally retarded, single-parent families, widowed, or newly married. The church that is sensitive to the aches and pains of its body will always have a vibrant ministry.

How to Solve People-Blindness

1.	Create a task force of members to brainstorm the potential community needs not being met by the church.
2.	Have the task force brainstorm possible programs to meet these needs.
3.	Study the "philosophy of ministry" in churches similar to yours that minister in neighborhoods similar to yours.
4.	Plan special Sunday School classes or Bible studies for "need" groups.
5.	Have the pastor preach on the definition of ministry, "communicating the gospel to people at their point of need."

Koinonitis

"Koinonitis" is the next disease that hinders church growth. This word is based on the Greek stem *koin* which is the root of the "fellowship" words in the New Testament. *Koinonia* is fellowship. But it is possible for a church to go to "seed" on fellowship. When the relationship among church members is so important that outreach is neglected, that church has a disease—koinonitis. Technically, koinonitis is inbred allegiance or fellowship with itself, and that becomes its unique commitment. The Great Commission is the aim of the church, but some groups have made other things the top priority. When secondary things (internal fellowship) become the primary test of Christianity, the church will have difficulty maintaining sustained growth.

	How to Solve Koinonitis
1.	Organize a "Friend Day" so that everyone is accountable to enroll a friend for attendance on a special day.
2.	Give everyone in the church a spiritual gifts inventory so that those with the gift of evangelism can be identified and involved in a weekly outreach program.
3.	Create new Bible study groups or adult Sunday School classes that will put new members and old members on an equal basis, hence making it possible to bond new members to the church.
4.	The pastor must create an "outreach attitude" from the pulpit that focuses the initiative of the congregation on the unchurched.
5.	Create a follow-up program to bond visitors to the church.

Sociological Strangulation

A fifth disease hindering church growth has been called "sociological strangulation." This refers to the situation where the physical facilities (church sanctuary and classrooms) are not capable of providing for growth. Just as you can't pour 12 ounces of milk into a 6-ounce glass without spilling it, so you can't get 200 people in a church that is designed for 100 people. They will spill over. And like spilt milk that is lost, some people visit the overcrowded church and never return. Then we cry over spilt milk.

As a rule of thumb, when the pews are 80 percent full, the church will not grow. Churches are like a box of corn flakes; you never get a full box, you have to allow for settlement. This rule cannot be reversed. Space will not make a church grow, but lack of space will keep it from growing. The church must offer a dynamic outreach of the gospel to produce growth.

Sociological strangulation also applies to the parking lot. In our day of convenience-market mentality and fast-food frenzy, people will go only where there is a place for them to park. This principle applies to the church as well. There is a correlation between the number of parking spaces and church growth.

Solving Sociological Strangulation	
1.	Begin a second worship service.
2.	Move adult Sunday School classes off the church campus to local restaurants, banquet rooms at a hotel/motel, homes, or rooms provided for public service.
3.	Begin a youth worship service to give more room for adults. (This is going to two worship services.)
4.	Make a long-range plan to construct new facilities.
5.	Bring in a consultant to guide the church in solving the space problem

Arrested Spiritual Development

A sixth church growth disease has been called "arrested spiritual development." When a church stops growing internally, it ultimately stops growing externally. Lack of prayer, lack of Bible study, and no vision arrest spiritual development. Internal growth (growth in grace) becomes the foundation for numerical growth.

Healing Arrested Spiritual Growth	
1.	Conduct a stewardship campaign to teach church members biblical stewardship of time, talents, and treasure.
2.	Pastors should address known cases of unconfessed sin among members personally and (if necessary) publicly.
3.	Organize the church to pray for the resolution of church problems and needs of the community.
4.	Conduct a Friend Day campaign to motivate church members to reach out beyond themselves to the lost in their sphere of influence.
5.	Institute new times/meetings for prayer and intercession. If the traditional prayer meeting has lost its vitality, perhaps a series of early morning prayer meetings before members go to work will revitalize the church.

St. John's Syndrome

The seventh church growth disease is "St. John's Syndrome." This condition occurs during a transition from the first generation to the second generation. First generation members are usually pioneers who want to expand the church, and second generation church members are usually settlers who want to settle down on the land.

The term St. John refers to the author of the Book of Revelation who describes the church at Ephesus. This church left its first love, Jesus Christ (Rev. 2:4). When a church leaves its love for Christ as expressed in soul-winning and teaching the Word of God, it has St. John's Syndrome.

Solving St. John's Syndrome	
1.	Organize a task force to examine the mission (objectives) of the church with a view of analyzing its effectiveness in mission.

2.	Plan a Friend Day that will lead the church into an organized outreach campaign.
3.	Organize new Bible study classes/cells to reach and bond new members into the church.
4.	The pastor should bring a series of messages on the mission of the church, along with suggestions to involve more members in ministry.

Hypopneumia

"Hypopneumia" is a church disease caused by a subnormal level of the presence and power of the Holy Spirit in the life and ministry of the church. Some call this being dead in Christ, while others call it backsliding. Whatever the symptoms, the church needs renewal and revival so that it returns to its original place of walking with God and experiencing the power of God.

How to Solve Hypopneumia	
1.	Organize and begin prayer meetings to intercede for revival.
2.	Church leaders attend meetings that are designed to renew their spiritual life and work.
3.	Invite speakers to challenge the church to spirituality.
4.	Repent of the sin of formalism and inactivity.
5.	Seek God's presence in the church.

Types of Growth

Obviously, this book is about numerical growth. It is about breaking the 100 barrier, the 400 barrier, and the 1,000 barrier. But you can never get numerical growth alone and remain a church. Because the church is a body, it has interrelated life-support systems that depends on the health and functions of all organs for the whole to grow and be healthy. A church must be healthy in all areas to be a growing body of interdependent members. "There are many parts of our bodies, so it is with Christ's body. We are all parts of it, and it takes everyone of us to make it complete for we each have different work to do" (Rom. 12:5 LB).

Many kinds of growth contribute to the total health of the church body. Church growth leaders use the following list to identify types of growth:

Internal Growth—when Christians grow or a church grows in grace and knowledge of the Lord. This is also described as nurture.

External Growth—this is numerical growth in attendance, offerings, membership, or enrollment.

Biological Growth—this is numerical growth through babies being born to church members and added to the church.

Transfer Growth—this involves Christians of "like faith and like practice" who join a church. Since 22 percent of Americans move to new homes each year, churches should target displaced Christians in their outreach programs. This is not sheep stealing; it is finding lost sheep.

Conversion Growth—this is numerical growth by winning lost people to Jesus Christ and bonding them to the church.

To Take Away

The prayer of the authors is that all churches would grow and carry out the Great Commission. When that happens, God is glorified. Our mentor, Donald McGavran, loved to quote the manifestation of the Great Commission in Romans 15, because it included the words *panta ta ethne*, "unto all people groups." This is our prayer. "This is God's plan of salvation for you Gentiles, kept secret from the beginning of time. But now as the prophets foretold and as God commands, this message is being preached everywhere, so that people around the world will have faith in Christ and obey Him. To God alone who is wise, be glory forever through Jesus Christ Our Lord" (Rom. 16:26,27 LB).

A friend once told a pastor whose church once averaged over 1,000 in attendance, that when he limited his outreach, he limited his ministry, and when he limited his ministry, he limited his church.

This book is the product of many who have taught us much about church growth. We thank God for every pastor who has broken growth barriers. May many others follow their example.

We give credit for this book to all our mentors—pastors, leaders, and lay church workers—who have taught us much about church growth. At the same time, we take all responsibility for the omissions, misconceptions, and faults of this book. Our prayer is that God would use it for his glory.

Sincerely yours in Christ,
Elmer, Peter, and Thom
Summer 1998

PART 1

OVERCOMING SMALL CHURCH

BARRIERS OF 200 PEOPLE

BY

C. PETER WAGNER

C. Peter Wagner has never stopped learning since he began. He learned a scientific orientation to growth at Rutgers University, Camden, New Jersey, majoring in agricultural studies. After graduation from Fuller Theological Seminary, he ministered for sixteen years in Bolivia, directing the mission that is now called Andean field of SIM International. After a sabbatical back at Fuller in 1968, he became a lifelong friend and student of Donald C. McGavran. Peter was invited to teach at Fuller in 1971, and he completed a Ph.D. in anthropology at the University of Southern California. McGavran and Wagner made Fuller the world leader in the Church Growth Movement, and to know the movement, one had to study there.

Wagner has authored many of the foundational classics in Church Growth. His research has both deepened the movement in foundational studies and broadened the movement, especially in his research into new movements of the Holy Spirit in prayer and spiritual warfare.

C. Peter Wagner holds the Donald C. McGavran Chair of Church Growth and Missions at Fuller and is the Dean of the Colorado Extension of Fuller. But close to his heart is the work of the World Prayer Center in Colorado Springs, Colorado, where he is the director. He has been on the cutting edge, writing several volumes on prayer and spiritual warfare.

Peter is married to Doris, who was instrumental in leading him to Christ. She was an effective missionary with him in South America and has developed an extensive prayer ministry around the world. They have three daughters and six grandchildren.

CHAPTER ONE

Why Do Churches
Face a 200 Barrier?

Over 90 percent of pastors here in America and around the world have come head-to-head with the 200 barrier. Very few have overcome this challenge. The great majority, however, have treated this challenge as passively as never running a four-minute mile, never being invited to the White House, or never owning a Mercedes. Nice, but that's what other people do.

Though most pastors probably don't think about breaking the 200 barrier very often, they do think about it from time to time. The very fact that you have opened this book shows that, at least now, you are thinking about it. It goes without saying that if you are ever going to break the 200 barrier, you have already taken a good first step. By the time you read these first three chapters you will be well on your way.

Why a Section on the 200 Barrier?

Breaking the 200 barrier is the top agenda item of most pastors who have a heartfelt desire for church growth. It is not that important for all pastors, of course, because many pastors care little or nothing about growth. This book is obviously not for them. But why start a book on plateaued churches with the 200 barrier?

First of all, the 200 barrier is important because "expansion growth" is a part of the job description, either implicitly or explicitly, of those pastors who do care about growth. Expansion growth is a technical term describing the process of bringing new members into your local church. It is different from "internal growth" (helping believers mature in their Christian life), "extension growth" (planting new churches in one's own culture), and "bridging growth" (planting churches in different cultures). The chances are that you and your church members want to see your church growing in numbers.

Second, the vast majority of pastors everywhere have congregations of fewer than 200 active members. More than half of these pastor fewer than 100 active members. Because of that, some may well be asking why we do not start with breaking the 100 barrier instead of breaking the 200 barrier. That is a good question. The answer is that the same essential characteristics of this barrier are largely present in all churches with membership under 200. For years I have been doing a seminar on this challenging subject I now call "Breaking the 100/200 Barrier." In the beginning I called it "Breaking the 200 Barrier," but I soon discovered that many pastors whose churches had fewer than 100 members were staying away for the wrong reasons. Later on I will explain these numbers in considerable detail, but for now let me simply say that any church under 200 falls into the category of a small church.

Most practicing pastors, therefore, are small-church pastors. A considerable number of these pastors are asking: "How can my church become a middle-sized church or a large church?" This entire book is designed to give you realistic and practical answers to that extremely important question.

What I Hope to Do for You

In this section of the book, I hope to help you with five highly valuable pieces of information directly connected to your leadership and ministry.

1. I want to help you recognize that a 200 barrier actually exists. This is not some kind of a slogan or rhetoric for a sermon point or figment of someone's imagination. It is almost as inexorable as the law of gravity. As astronauts know, humans can be exempt from the law of gravity at certain times and in certain places. Likewise, some megachurch pastors may never have been bothered with a 200 barrier. But astronauts and megachurch pastors are few and far between.

2. I want to help you understand why that 200 barrier exists. This is not a mystery that has to keep you puzzled all your life. The reality is that certain predictable sociological, psychological, behavioral, and spiritual factors combine to make people actually prefer their churches to have memberships of under 200 active adults. You will soon understand what these mind-sets are.

3. Once you thoroughly understand the nature of the 200 barrier, I want to help you make a realistic assessment as to whether your particular church has a high probability or a low probability of ever breaking the barrier. This assessment is very important, because not every church can or will be able to do it. I refuse to engage in the kind of hype that implies that if you just do 1, 2, and 3 or if you get your spiritual act together or if you read this book, your church will certainly break the 200 barrier. A message like that puts you in the position of blaming only yourself if your church does not

break the 200 barrier. In some cases the blame will clearly be yours, but not in every case.

By the time you finish reading this book, you certainly will be well-informed, and you may honestly be saying to yourself, to your spouse, and to God: "No way! This church will never break the 200 barrier!" If that turns out to be the case, then your options are very simple. You can decide to stay where you are and be a small-church pastor for the rest of your life. This may well be God's will for you and your family. If it is, frustration will evaporate because you will thoroughly understand why the church remains the size it is, and you will be comforted to know that in most cases it is not because of anything you have done wrong. Be a good small-church pastor. The other option, of course, is to send out your resume and look up U-Haul in the yellow pages.

4. On the other hand, if you finish this book and find yourself saying, "Yes! We can do it!" I want to help you comprehend as thoroughly as possible the dynamics of what you will have to do to break the 200 barrier.

5. Finally, I want to provide you with some practical conceptual tools you can use to implement the process. I do not intend to give you some tried-and-true formula for growth, because I don't think any such thing exists. Breaking the 200 barrier will hardly ever be easy, but let's try to make it as easy as possible.

This Definitely Can Work

As I have led 200-barrier seminars over the years, I have received many responses from pastors who have tried what my colleagues and I have suggested, and it has worked. Here are some samples.

A Baptist pastor from West Virginia writes: "It has been just under a year since I attended your seminar. Some very encouraging things have happened in our church. I believe a great deal of our recent success can be attributed to the skills and insights gained in the seminar. For the first quarter of this year, our average attendance in morning worship was 289 compared with 197 last year. Our Sunday School has gone from 154 to 185."

A pastor from Texas writes: "I just wanted to drop you a note to let you know how much your seminar helped us. We had been between 130 and 160 for over a year. We came home and began to apply some of the principles we learned at the seminar. I'm happy to report that we have broken the 200 barrier!"

I love this letter from a pastor in Oregon: "The church I serve was running 200 to 225 for three years until I attended the seminar. The seminar was so liberating to me—it totally changed my ministry philosophy. In the last two years we have grown to over 400!"

Looking at Small Churches

There are two principal ways of looking at small churches. One is from the point of view of maintenance, and the other is from the point of view of growth.

Both of these approaches are legitimate. Books on maintenance are valuable, and I will quote from some of them in my chapters. But my focus in this book is not on maintenance; it is on growth. I like what Rick Warren says about church growth: "Since the church is a living organism, it is natural for it to grow if it is healthy. The church is a body, not a business. It is an organism, not an organization. It is alive. If a church is not growing, it is dying."[1] Well, maybe not exactly dying, maybe just surviving. There are churches in my rural hometown in upstate New York that have not grown for 100 years, but they are not dead yet. However, I can't say they are healthy.

In any case, many churches that are living organisms and should be growing have been plateaued at under 200 members for too long a time. In those cases, the major function of this book will be to help leaders identify and remove obstacles to growth. When it comes right down to it, that is all we can do. We don't grow the church, God does. Paul said, "I have planted, Apollos watered, but God gave the increase" (1 Cor. 3:6 KJV). Growth can happen as we increase our ability to diagnose the health of our churches and work on curing any growth-obstructing diseases.

Three books on the *growth* of small churches have attracted my attention the most. I will come to books on *maintenance* later. The books I like the best are: *Get Ready . . . Get Set . . . Grow!* by Gary W. Exman; *Ten Steps to Breaking* the *200 Barrier* by Bill M. Sullivan; and *Turn Around Strategies for the Small Church* by Ron Crandall. Since most rural churches are small, another excellent book on that subject is *The Lord's Harvest and the Rural Church* by Kent R. Hunter. All four authors are my personal friends, and they have firsthand experience in dealing positively with small churches.

Quantifying Growth Barriers

Several researchers have recognized the existence of predictable, numerical barriers to growth. Notice especially the adjectives *predictable* and *numerical.* What this means is that a certain *number* of people in a church can, in itself, cause a slowdown of growth. This is not only true of the 200 barrier, but of other numerical barriers as well, as you will see later on in this book. The question does not necessarily involve the *quality* of the people, as some may wish to suggest. How much the church members pray or how holy they are or how many verses of the Bible they can quote or how much of their income they give to the church are important characteristics for believers, but in regard to church growth they are not very relevant. What counts is how many people are involved. This principle would apply as much to Christian Scientists or Jehovah's Witnesses as it would to Methodists or Assemblies of God.

First of all, let's look at the numbers themselves. Renowned parish consultant Lyle Schaller, looking at worship attendance, gives 35, 75, 140, 200, 350, 600, and 700+ as the potential numerical barriers.[2] David A. Womack of the Assemblies of God, counting believers, says that organizational shifts are needed at 50, 90, 120, 250–300, 600, and 1,200.[3] William C. Tinsley uses worship attendance as does Schaller, and he comes up with 40, 100, 250, 500, and 1,000 as predictable barriers to growth.[4]

As these expert researchers and others have examined numerous churches, discerning certain numerical barriers to growth, some of them have also ventured to attach descriptive terms to churches in each of the resulting categories. I think it is very instructive to peruse the terminology they have developed. In fact, I suggest you read over two or three times the list on page 30 because they will leave a very useful deposit in your mind.

In my opinion, the best book to help us understand the internal dynamics of the small church was written twenty years ago by Carl Dudley, who now teaches at Hartford Seminary. Many good books on the small church have been published since then, but Dudley's has not been surpassed. The fact of the matter is that small churches are not much different today than they were twenty years ago! In this book, *Making the Small Church Effective,* Dudley focuses on maintenance; the book is not about growth. Naturally, Dudley defines precisely what he means by a small church and gives some numbers. However, one of his very important concepts is: "small is something more than a numerical description."[5] The implication is that *smallness is essentially a state of mind.* Very well put!

Carl Dudley continues, "But small churches are unique. They are not multicelled organizations with a common base. Small churches are a single, caring cell embracing the whole congregation."[6] Almost everything I say in the rest of this chapter will be an elaboration of this crucial point.

Dudley gives only two numbers to define a small church; both are related to what I have just quoted. His dividing line for a small

Lyle Schaller (worship attendance)	
35	fellowship group
75	small church
140	middle-sized church
200	awkward-sized church
350	large church
600	huge church
700+	minidenomination[7]

William Tinsley (worship attendance)	
40 ±10	core group
100 ±20	congregational church
250 ±50	multicongregational church
500 ±100	polycongregational church
1000 ±200	megacongregational church[8]

Douglas Walrath (resident members)	
75	very small congregation
75–200	small congregation
200–350	middle-sized congregation
350–750	moderately large congregation
750+	very large congregation[9]

church is 250. He doesn't state exactly what the number 250 represents, but it is safe to assume that 250 refers to the regular membership constituency of the church. His descriptive terms are very helpful for future reference.

Just as a note of interest, some readers might be wondering if any such thing as a "metachurch" exists, since at the present time

Carl Dudley

Fewer than 250	single-celled church
250 or more	multicelled church

As I have studied and taught on these terms over the years, I have decided to develop my own range of size and descriptive terminology for each one. My numbers refer to active adults.

Peter Wagner (active adults)

40-80	fellowship group
200 and less	small church
150–350	awkward size (Schaller's term)
400–750	large church
750–2,000	superchurch
2,000–20,000	megachurch
20,000 +	metachurch

no churches in the United States or Canada have a membership exceeding 20,000. Yes, these churches exist. They are located in Asia, Africa, and Latin America. On a recent trip to Korea, for example, I was conversing with Myung Sung Hoon, who is considered to be Mr. Church Growth of Korea, and he matter-of-factly mentioned in passing a certain "moderate-sized church of 10,000!" On that trip I spoke in one church of 700,000, two of 80,000, and one of 60,000.

This section of the book deals with the 150–350 range, which Lyle Schaller first called the "awkward size," a perfect description. It also includes churches in the 80–150 range, which face many of the same dynamics of the awkward churches and will have to solve the problems involved if they are ever to break the 200 barrier.

The 200 Barrier

Now we are ready to define as precisely as possible just exactly what the 200 barrier is. First, make no mistake that the 200 barrier is by far the most consistent and predictable of all the numerical barriers we have reviewed. The essential reason for this is, using Carl Dudley's terminology, *crossing the 200 barrier represents the transition from the single cell to a multicelled church.* In many denominations over 90 percent of the local churches have not crossed the 200 barrier. A few denominations come in at a bit less than 90 percent. Among the lowest are Lutheran Church-Missouri Synod, Evangelical Free Church, and Reformed Church in America with 72 percent each.[10]

Secondly, 200 means 200 active adults. One of the interesting phenomena of our day is that many pastors now choose not to count "members" of their churches. On numerous occasions I have asked pastors how many members they have, and they have replied, "None!" This is a surprising response for those of us who are traditionalists, but it turns out that they have well thought-out reasons (which I will not go into here) for their position. But they will respond when asked, "How many adults do you have in your constituency?" or, "How many people consider your church their primary source of spiritual nourishment?" or other words to that effect.

Now the number 200 should not be taken as a precisely fixed number. It is the median point in a range that runs from approximately 150 to 250. Some churches have a certain combination of other growth factors that allow the 200 barrier to reach 250 before it begins to stall out. This was the case of the Oregon pastor whose letter I quoted earlier. His church had regular attendance of 200–225. He undoubtedly had more than 225 active adults in the church.

Other churches have different growth factors that cause them to buck up against the 200 barrier at around 150. Your five-year graph of growth will show this in most cases. The top of your graph will be jagged. It will go up until it hits your barrier level, be it 150, 200, 250, or whatever; then it will go down temporarily and start up again. Incidentally, such a graph can be a very valuable instrument as you present what you learn in this book to your church leaders.

Why would I say that even a church of 100 or slightly fewer can be at the 200 barrier? Because the mention of such a number makes many church leaders think attendance rather than active adults. Suppose a church plateaus at the lower end of the 200 barrier range, namely 150 active adults. Usually, everyone does not attend church on a given Sunday, meaning that attendance in such a church might be running around 100. This church could well be at the 200 barrier.

Why Do Most Churches Remain under 200?

Clearly, the majority of churches never grow to more than 200. The Church Growth Movement seeks to find the answers to the obvious question: Why? We, the authors, approach such questions with an admitted bias. We are not among those sociologists whose goal is to conduct value-free research for the sake of reporting good research to our academic colleagues. Our goal is to extend the kingdom of God. We believe God wants his lost sheep found, and he wants every church to be winning lost people to Christ, adding them to their fold, and consequently growing. Healthy churches should be growing. If a church is not growing, it is sick for some reason or another. If it is, let's find out what is wrong and, if the particular disease is curable, let's cure the illness!

Jesus' Great Commission to spread his gospel to every nation and people group throughout the world constituted his final words on earth (see Acts 1:8). Elmer Towns, Thom S. Rainer, and I feel that they are among his most important words, and we have given our lives to do our part in helping to fulfill that Great Commission. How will we go about getting this job done? We will do whatever it takes. Throughout the years we have regularly been accused of being "pragmatic," as if pragmatism were some sin that we need to confess. Accusing church growth leaders of being pragmatic would be like accusing the pope of being Catholic. Part of our whatever-it-takes approach is to be very realistic about growth-inhibiting church diseases.

One of my latest books on this subject is *The Healthy Church,* in which I carefully describe what I have found to be the most prominent of the growth-inhibiting church diseases. I highly recommend it as a supplement to this book. In *The Healthy Church* I have chapters on seven curable diseases and how to diagnose and cure them. But I also have two chapters on terminal illnesses. I realize that it comes as somewhat a surprise to many when they hear that churches can contract terminal illnesses. But they obviously can, as is witnessed by the fact that so many of them die each year. If your church does have a terminal illness, the sooner you find out about it the better. If you find out soon enough, you can make plans to die with dignity! Most churches don't, and they tend to die kicking and screaming.

Decide Whether Your Church Can Break the 200 Barrier

The first step toward approaching the possibility of breaking the 200 barrier is to determine whether your church might be afflicted with either of the two terminal illnesses. If so, the probability is that your church can never get past 200. I say "probability" because God is still on the throne, and He is a healing God. I am in touch with documented cases of cancer, which have been medically diagnosed as terminal and have been remitted through prayer without a trace. If this can happen to a terminally ill person, it can also happen to a church. But, let's face reality: most terminally ill cancer patients die of the disease.

I will summarize the two terminal illnesses here. Both of these illnesses are caused by *contextual* factors as opposed to the seven curable diseases, which are all caused by *institutional* factors. Contextual factors are sociological factors the church cannot change or control, despite the fact that they greatly influence whether a church will grow. Institutional factors are ecclesiastical factors the church can change or control if it desires to do so. Because the two terminal illnesses are contextual, it is important, and at times comforting, to know that neither one has been caused by anything the pastor or the congregation did. The appropriate response is not guilt or casting blame.

Ethnikitis

"Ethnikitis" is the church disease caused by a changing community. It is almost always an urban disease. The most susceptible churches are neighborhood churches, as contrasted, for example, to central-city old first churches or metropolitan regional churches. Typically, the church will draw its members from the surrounding neighborhood. Then, *due to circumstances beyond the control of the church,* the neighborhood begins to change. Those who have populated the neighborhood for years begin to move to other neighborhoods. People from other ethnic, socio-economic, language, national, or educational backgrounds begin to move in. As the neighborhood continues to change (the rate of change will vary from place to place), the typical church becomes a congregation of commuters who used to live in the neighborhood and senior citizens who cannot afford to move. The church is like an island in a sea of a different people group to whom it has few or no ministry bridges to offer. With a rare but notable exception (usually when the pastor has the missionary gift), a church that fits this description will never break the 200 barrier because its days as a church are numbered.

Ghost Town Disease

The second terminal illness that may afflict churches is Ghost Town Disease. Ghost Town Disease is caused by a *deteriorating* community rather than a *changing* community. People are moving out, but few are moving in. It is mostly a rural disease. The day of the family farm is virtually gone. Young people leave town for school, get married, and only return for holidays. Businesses close and schools merge to form unified school districts. Some rural communities give up the ghost. Others survive, with a steadily climbing age profile. Churches begin closing their doors. Some, which may have picked up an endowment over the years, will survive. However, most will die of Ghost Town Disease after a period of survival, short or long, on the functional equivalent of life-support systems. None can be expected to break the 200 barrier.

Five Institutional Factors
Creating a 200 Barrier

Institutional factors are those that can be determined by the action of the pastor or the congregation. Growing churches invariably are characterized by a combination of positive institutional factors. But they are not all that positive. I have found five institutional factors to be especially determinative in creating a 200 barrier. Almost every church leader who has been wrestling with the 200 barrier for a period of time will immediately recognize that these factors exist, and that they can be extremely powerful in keeping a small church small. One reason they are so powerful is, with the exception of blaming them for a low level of evangelistic zeal, none of these factors is in itself bad, sinful, wicked, or malicious.

Putting these five factors together, it is easy to see why almost all churches have a membership under 200. In one sense, it is *natural* for a church to have fewer than 200 members. Perhaps the church might not be very *healthy*, as we have noted, but it is doing what seems to come naturally. I will present these factors briefly at this point because the rest of my section builds from them in more detail.

1. The Desire to Preserve Social Intimacy

Here is what Carl Dudley says: "The basic obstacle to growth [in the small church] lies in the satisfactions of the present church membership. When the church is seen as one caring cell the problem is neither complex nor judgmental. The small church is already the right size for everyone to know, or know about, everyone else. This intimacy is not an accident. The essential character of the small church is this capacity to care about people personally. The small church cannot grow in membership size without giving up its most precious appeal, its intimacy."[11]

Of all the institutional factors, this is the most crucial. Notice Dudley's operative words: *essential character* and *intimacy*. In the minds of almost all small-church members, personal intimacy is what belonging to church is all about.

2. The Desire to Maintain Control

The small church usually has one power center. Sometimes it is as small as one person. Sometimes it is a family. Sometimes it is a clique. Identifying the power center can be tricky because it is frequently located in the informal leadership structure of the church rather than in the formal structure of established boards and committees. No matter how large or where it might be located, typically the individuals who constitute the power center have gained their power over a considerable period of time and with what they consider to be a considerable amount of personal sacrifice. Once they have attained the power, they have decided that they like it and want to keep it. They have no interest in ever seeing their small church become a larger church because they intuitively know that if the church grows they could lose their power.

Many of these power-center leaders have perfected a fail-safe device to ensure their continued powerful influence in the church, that is, to change their pastor every three or four years. Research has shown that the effective years of pastoral ministry in an established church *begin* between years three and six, so this method assures that no pastor will be truly effective and either assume power or reshape the power center. A by-product of this revolving door is that without effective pastoral leadership scarcely any church could possibly pass the 200 barrier.

3. The Desire to Conserve Memories

This factor kicks in particularly when, as in many cases, a new meeting place will be necessary for the church to break the 200 barrier. Many church members can become very emotional over the physical church building and sanctuary because it holds so many memories for them. Here is where we were married. Here is where my uncle and aunt were baptized. My mother and father sat right over there in the second pew. Think of Edward's funeral and how practically the whole town crowded in that morning. Our children were born again in those Sunday School rooms downstairs.

Thoughts of leaving this place are out of the question. Even fiery sermons on outreach and evangelism do not usually change this strong, emotional feeling.

4. The Desire to Protect Turf

Even though this factor is hardly ever vocalized, the mind-set of many influential persons in a small church is: "New people are a threat to what we have worked so hard to obtain."

I love the way Lyle Schaller expresses this mind-set. He writes:

> The strong commitment of the members to one another, to kinfolk ties, to the meeting place, to the concept that the congregation should function as one big family, and the modest emphasis on program tend to reinforce the single-cell character of the small church. When combined with the intergenerational nature of the typical long-established small

church, these forces tend to enhance the caring nature of the fellowship, but at the cost of potential numerical growth .

These unifying principles tend to make the small church an exclusionary institution. While there usually is not a conscious effort to exclude strangers, their expressions of institutional commitment tend to make it difficult for the small-membership church to reach, attract, and assimilate potential new members, unless people have kinfolk in that congregation.[12]

5. The Desire to Remain Comfortable

Let's face it. Change is a threat. Since growth implies change, church growth can be a threat. Carl Dudley writes: "But the small church must be 'converted' to believe that the change is worth the cost. One pastor at a conference on methods of evangelism observed that 'any of these methods, if used conscientiously, would turn the small church into a large church, and *that's the one thing most small congregations don't want to see happen* [emphasis mine].' Members of the small church know the alternatives."[13]

While Lyle Schaller's *The Small Church Is Different* is a book on maintenance, one of his other excellent books on growth is *44 Ways to Increase Church Attendance.* In the introduction to the book, Schaller, with a characteristic touch of humor, writes: "The most persuasive argument against reading this book can be summarized in eight terrifying words. *What if we try it and it* works? If a congregation tries a new approach to ministry and it fails, little harm is done. Usually everything soon returns to the way it was before, and life goes on. The great risk is to implement a new idea that may work. If it does, the world will never be the same again!"[14]

Most people are comfortable with the world in which they now live. If some other church wants to experiment with a new world, fine. I like our church the size it is!

What Is the Right Size?

Why would so many people prefer a small church to a larger one? I'm sure many readers will be surprised when I agree with Carl Dudley, whom I quoted earlier as saying, "The small church is already the right size."[15] Let me explain.

Have you ever heard of the "Rule of Forty"? This is one of Lyle Schaller's contributions. He claims that this is one of the most neglected rules of church administration. He writes: "In general, whenever human beings gather in a voluntary association that emphasizes relationships with one another, there is a natural tendency to limit the size to fewer than 40 persons. Illustrations are numerous. Throughout history, all military organizations have limited the basic unit to fewer than 40. Major league baseball teams limit a team's roster to 40 in the winter and 25 after the season begins. The Lion's Club that wins the regional attendance award usually has fewer than 40 members. One-fourth of all Protestant congregations in North America average fewer than 35 in Sunday worship."[16]

The Church Growth Research Center of the Church of the Nazarene, which conducted a study of congregations with 30–50 in worship in 1985, reported, "It is tough for a small congregation to grow past 50 or 60 in attendance" and discovered that, five years later, fewer than one in ten had as many as 60 in worship. They concluded: "Churches that have been under 50 for five years are likely to remain about that size for the next five."[17]

What is the reason for these numbers? It is very simple. When church membership is under 40, every member is aware of every other member. Over a reasonable period of time, all members can learn the names of the others, and they can work together efficiently. A frequently unrecognized advantage of this group size over a home cell of, say, 8 to 12, is that every member does not have to be particularly fond of every other member for the group to function.

It should also be noted that churches of around 40, give or take, were the rule in New Testament times. Churches met for weekly times of worship and fellowship in private homes. Each one was led by one or more elders. Sometimes we superimpose our own church experience on something like "the church of God which is in Corinth" (1 Cor. 1:2 KJV) and imagine that every Sunday all the believers in Corinth got together in a worship center to hear the same preacher deliver the same sermon. But such was not the case. When Paul went to Miletus and called a conference for "the elders of the church" of Ephesus (Acts 20:17 NIV), he was inviting the pastors of the various congregations that regularly met in homes. Few of the homes in Ephesus would have held more than 40 at a time.

Moving Beyond Forty

Let's suppose that winning new people to Christ is a high priority for our "ideal-sized" church of 40. Let's suppose that the 40 becomes 80. Eighty is twice the ideal size, but it can work. At 80, not everyone will know everyone else's name, but they learn to live with it. It is still a single-cell church that is functioning quite well.

Now let's suppose that new people are still coming to Christ and into membership in the church, and the church grows to between 80 and 200. It is now oversized. It has become a saturated solution. I well remember when, in chemistry class in high school, we each took a glass of water and stirred salt into it. The salt disappeared. We kept putting more salt into the glass until suddenly no more salt would disappear because it became a saturated solution. This is exactly what churches of 80 to 200 tend to become.

Carl Dudley describes this well when he says, "Small-church members unconsciously feel that they cannot absorb new members without changing the fabric of the group. According to the experts in group relations, the small church is already much larger than similar kinds of caring groups. Members often feel the strain. They feel that they cannot receive new members without losing touch with those whom they already know. *They cannot make a radical change in the size of the church without losing their motivation for belonging* [emphasis mine]. . . They cannot grow because, in a word, they feel 'stuffed.'"[18]

Is Growth Possible?

In this chapter I have done my best to help you understand the nature of the 200 barrier and why the great majority of churches find themselves under it. But this is not a book on information, nor does it intend to perpetuate the under 200 comfort zone. It is a book on fulfilling Jesus' Great Commission and, therefore, a book on growth and breaking church growth barriers. If there are unsaved people in your community, your church should be doing its part to reach them and win them to Christ. I will now move on to describe what needs to be done if your church is one of those destined to break the 200 barrier.

CHAPTER TWO

The Cost of Breaking
the 200 Barrier

If so many people feel that somewhere around 40, possibly stretching it to 80, is the best size for a church, it is patently obvious that in order for churches to get past the 200 barrier, something in the hearts and minds of the church members has to change. In other words, if a church is going to grow numerically, it must be motivated to grow. Motivation for growth is the first step toward breaking the 200 barrier.

Pumping Water Uphill

Lyle Schaller agrees with the premise stated above. To lay the groundwork for a major point, he says, "One of the concepts that had a very negative impact on the United States Army in Vietnam was the declaration that 'every second lieutenant is a potential future chief of staff.' A parallel concept that can be equally destructive is for denominational leaders to perceive every small congregation as a future thousand-member church." Then comes his major point: "To produce congregations larger than [40 people] is like pumping water uphill. It can be done, but it means opposing the forces of nature and requires persistent and continuous effort."[1]

This is a great analogy. If you took a shower this morning, you did so only because someone went to the pain of pumping some water uphill. Pumping water uphill can be done, and it has become so routine in our daily lives that we hardly even think of it unless someone like Lyle Schaller mentions it. But pumping water uphill can't be taken for granted; the minute someone fails to take responsibility for getting our water pumped uphill, there are no more showers. Left to the forces of nature alone, we would all be bathing in the river, as millions of people in more primitive societies still do today.

The same principle applies to church growth. Left to the forces of ecclesiastical nature, hardly any church would break the 200 barrier. But we can, and in most cases we should, do whatever it takes to oppose the sociological and psychological mind-sets that work to keep churches small and evangelistically impotent.

The Starting Point:
Motivation

No church I know of has grown without being motivated to grow. Two targets are necessary for this motivation: the pastor and the people. Although I have been asked the question many times, I have never been able to say which one is the most important. I believe that the responsibility for growth is 50 percent the pastor and 50 percent the people. I remember, however, that I once said this to a group of Korean pastors, and one responded, "I don't think it is 50–50. I think it is 51 percent the pastor and 49 percent the people."

I think I understand what he was saying. I'm still sticking to my 50–50, but the point is that you cannot change the order. It is the pastor first, then the people. The motivation for church growth begins with God, and it is ordinarily transmitted by the Holy Spirit through the pastor to the congregation. Only in the rarest of occasions does growth motivation originate with the congregation for the reasons I spelled out in the last chapter.

Desire + Commitment = Motivation

Motivation is generated by a combination of desire and commitment. In the small church hoping to make it through the 200 barrier, both the pastor and the people must have these qualities.

The desire, if it is produced by the Holy Spirit, takes biblical root in both the Great Commission and the Great Commandment, two of the most important directives Jesus Christ gave to his followers, the church.

The Great Commission, which appears in all four gospels as well as in the Book of Acts, is summarized in Matthew 28:19–20: "Go therefore and make disciples of all the nations, baptizing them in the name of the Father and of the Son and of the Holy Spirit, teaching them to observe all things that I have commanded you" (NKJV). From Acts we learn that "all nations" includes Jerusalem, Judea, Samaria, and the uttermost parts of the earth (Acts 1:8 NKJV). Our equivalent of "Jerusalem" is our town or city or neighborhood or primary social circle. If we are obedient Christians, we will do what it takes to reach our lost neighbors and bring them into God's family, the church.

The Great Commandment is, "You shall love your neighbor as yourself" (Matt. 22:39 NASB). Do you feel that you and your family are benefiting from your relationship to God? Does your church make a positive contribution to your life and well-being? Would you feel deprived if God and your church were taken away from you? I am asking these rhetorical questions simply to say that if you love your neighbor as yourself, you will not want your neighbor to be deprived of God and the church.

Just think what would happen if everyone in your church took these two biblical principles as guiding principles for their lives. The church's desire to grow would go off the charts!

Desire alone is not enough. Commitment must follow. While commitment emerges from desire, and not vice versa, it does not always follow. You can have desire without commitment. For example, I have always wanted to play the guitar, but I could never find the time to practice! So, unless things change, I'll never play the guitar because I'm not committed enough to pay the required price.

If your church is ever to break the 200 barrier, both the pastor and the people must have a desire for and commitment to growth. As I frequently say, the first two axioms of church growth are: (1) the pastor must want the church to grow and be willing to pay the price, and (2) the people must want the church to grow and be willing to pay the price.

The Cost of Commitment #1: The Pastor

For the next few pages I'm going to talk to pastors about the price they will need to pay if they are really committed to leading their church past the 200 barrier. I know from experience that some pastors will be saying, "I realize I should do that, and I could, but my people won't let me." Keep in mind that right after addressing the pastors, I'm going to talk to the laypeople, so I hope to cover those bases. If things are really going to happen in your church, it has to be 50 percent pastor and 50 percent people.

1. Assume the leadership of your church. The quality of pastoral leadership is the most important of all the institutional factors that contribute to the growth of a church. Over twenty years ago I wrote a book called *Your Church Can Grow: Seven Vital Signs of a Healthy Church.* The seven vital signs have been subjected to a number of validity tests by researchers in a variety of institutions. My first vital sign has been confirmed as the number one factor on every test that has been done. It states: "A pastor who is a possibility thinker and whose dynamic leadership has been used to catalyze the entire church into action for growth."[2]

This means that if you want your church to grow past the 200 barrier, you must decide that the buck stops here. I am among the strongest advocates of pastors delegating ministry responsibilities to others. But there are two things that a growth pastor cannot delegate: faith (or vision) and leadership. You cannot ask someone else to cast the vision for where God wants the church to go or ask someone else to lead the people in implementing the vision. You must do it.

This is not an easy price to pay because it involves risk. The growth or non-growth of the church depends primarily on you. The risk, therefore, is the risk of failure. I am not saying this in any kind of judgmental way, but the fact of the matter is that some pastors simply cannot handle, either emotionally or psychologically, the risk of failure. If that is the case, it is part of the profile of a small-church pastor.

Let me repeat in this chapter what I affirmed in the last chapter. There is nothing wrong with being a small-church pastor. God loves small-church pastors. For starters, look at how many of them he has made! Many who read this section will conclude that they, in all probability, are going to be small-church pastors for the rest of their lives. No problem! If God has called you and equipped you to be a small-church pastor, my best advice to you is to be a good one.

Others, however, will come to a different conclusion. They may have been small-church pastors up to now, but they will sense the Holy Spirit telling them that God wants them to be pastors of a medium-sized or a large church. If that is the case, your first step is to become the leader of the church. There is no other way. If you need help, I suggest you get in touch with John Maxwell's Injoy ministry for books, tapes, and seminars on church leadership. It is the best thing going right now.

2. Work hard. It almost goes without saying that it is harder work to pastor a large, growing church than it is to pastor a small, plateaued one. In fact, if the church is declining, the work presumably gets easier each year! Some pastors I know enjoy this kind of a situation, and they strive to maintain the status quo. However, sustained, dynamic church growth requires a willingness to work. Fortunately, most of the pastors I know are more than ready to pay this price, as long as they receive encouragement from tangible results.

Some pastors are workaholics who love work more than anything else, who may even make work a higher priority than family and hardly ever see a waking hour pass when they are not producing something. Yet their churches haven't grown in ten years. How can this be? The answer is that they might be working hard, but they are not working smart.

3. Work smart. The secret of working smart is very simple: major on the majors and minor on the minors. This is all well and good, but how can you know the difference between the two? Through learning and implementing sound principles of time management. Time management is a well-developed and extensive field with one starting point for everyone: the realization that, when it comes to time, God has dealt us all the same hand—24 hours a day and seven days a week. I often hear pastors say, "So-and-so has more time than I do." That cannot be right. It would be more accurate to say, "So-and-so manages his or her time better than I do." The implication? You can do a better job at time management and end up with more time to do what you feel best contributes to your current goals.

I do a much better job at time management than I used to. For one thing, I have reached what J. Robert Clinton, in his excellent book *The Making of a Leader,* calls "convergence." "In convergence," Clinton says, "God moves the leader into a role that matches his or her gift-mix and experience so that ministry is maximized. The leader . . . is freed from ministry for which he is not gifted or suited."[3] I am fully aware that convergence is an impossible dream for the typical small-church pastor who is expected to be all things to all people. But it is definitely something to aim for in the long term.

John Maxwell taught me something that was most helpful in moving me toward convergence. That is, the real question isn't whether your schedule is full or not. The real question is: Who fills my schedule? At one point in time I was letting other people fill much of my schedule, which meant that I was constantly adjusting to someone else's priorities. I was majoring on *their* majors, not mine. No longer. I am not a pastor, but if I were, I would take to heart another word of wisdom from John Maxwell: a well-managed pastor will spend 80 percent of the available time with 20 percent of the church members. Many pastors are bogged down because they are spending almost 100 percent of their time with the 80 percent of the members who promise a relatively low return for the investment.

As you fill your schedule, be sure you build in enough time for leisure. I once heard Rick Warren say that we should divert daily, withdraw weekly, and abandon annually. This is excellent advice, which I have remembered and tried to follow. A church should give a pastor a minimum paid vacation of two weeks, or better yet, according to studies on pastoral burnout, three weeks per year. In addition, the church should pay all expenses for the pastor to attend a continuing education event each year for at least one week. Churches that don't follow these minimal standards for vacation and continuing education are not meeting today's industry standards.

4. Add staff. I am going to elaborate on this point in the next chapter, but I did not want to omit it from this list. The truth of the matter is that some pastors are, by nature, loners. Thus, the addition of new staff members is not something they will cheerfully consider. This is another characteristic of the profile of a small-church pastor, and, if adding staff is a threat, there is little probability that the church will break the 200 barrier.

5. *Mobilize lay ministry.* Many small-church pastors are accustomed to doing virtually all the ministry of the church. In fact, the church members assume that this is why the pastor has been hired. The pastor is frequently called "the minister." This attitude toward ministry is precisely why many churches have never been able to break the 200 barrier.

Although some pastors can do all the ministry in a church quite readily, it is not so easy for many pastors to share the ministry with laypeople. Shared ministry frequently becomes one of the highest costs of deciding to commit the church to break the 200 barrier.

For those who desire to move in the direction of shared ministry, I highly recommend my book, *Your Spiritual Gifts Can Help Your Church Grow.* In fact, a new video seminar on spiritual gifts has just come out that will allow me to come into your church and teach your people what spiritual gifts are and how to discover them.

6. *Switch from the shepherd mode of pastoring to the rancher mode.* Of all the changes that need to be made in a small church if it is ever to cross the 200 barrier, two stand head and shoulders above the rest: (1) transitioning from a single-cell to a multicelled church, and (2) switching from the shepherd mode of pastoring to the rancher mode. Not only are these changes necessary, but they are particularly difficult because they are the two changes most predictably resisted by the majority of church members.

Many pastors have developed a family-style, one-on-one relationship with every person in the congregation. They know everyone's name, where they work, who their children are, where they live, and what their current problems happen to be. They visit their homes from time to time and go to the hospital when they are sick. This is the shepherd mode of pastoring, and it is functional up to the 200 barrier. But in order to break the 200 barrier, the pastor must shift from the shepherd mode to the rancher mode. In the rancher mode, the question is not whether the sheep are cared for, but rather, who cares for the sheep?

There are many ways of accomplishing this shift, but the bottom line is this: the pastor, who by now is presumably the leader of the church, must delegate the pastoral care ministry to others and supervise the work they do in order to maintain the highest quality possible.

The Cost of Commitment #2: The People

I know from experience that very few laypeople would ordinarily purchase or read a book on church growth like this one. But if the congregation is serious about its desire and commitment to break through the 200 barrier, at least all the church's opinion-makers should read this section. When I use the second person "you" in this section, I am speaking to laypeople. This is a checklist of some of the prices you will have to pay if you expect your church to grow.

1. Make your pastor the "tribal chief." The first item on this list matches the first item on the list of prices the pastor will have to pay for growth through the 200 barrier. No pastor can assume the leadership of the church unless there is mutual agreement with the congregation. Are you willing to allow your pastor to be the "tribal chief"? This language comes from Lyle Schaller (as does the "shepherd-rancher" language I have just used), who contrasts the "tribal chief" of a congregation to the "medicine man." He writes, "In long-established smaller congregations, which usually experience short pastorates, the minister may function as the medicine man, but all leadership responsibilities are retained by the council of elders."[4]

This shift represents a huge break from the tradition of most older churches. In fact, some denominational church polities have been designed to keep the pastor in the role of medicine man. One mainline denomination, which requires its local churches to be governed by an elected board of elders, until recently called those elected by the congregation "ruling elders," while the pastor was designed a "teaching elder." Other churches are not that blatant about it, but the result is the same. The pastor is not allowed to lead but is hired to carry out the religious duties of the congregation. This "medicine man" mentality is a major reason most congregations remain under 200, and if the church is to grow it must be changed.

2. Learn to behave like sheep. The New Testament was written in a sheep-herding culture in which everyone fully understood the relationship between the pastor and the sheep. They knew that at the beginning of the day the pastor decided the direction the sheep would go, when they would move from pasture to pasture, and when they would come back at night. No sheep were expected to make such decisions. The pastor was their leader.

This is the analogy Jesus used to describe the operation of the church. Consider these rhetorical questions: Q: Who owns the church? A: Jesus owns the church. Q: Who in a local church is the most directly accountable to Jesus? A: The pastor of the church. Jesus is the great Shepherd of the sheep (see Heb. 13:20), and his undershepherds are the pastors (see 1 Pet. 5:2–4). If Jesus returns today, the first person he will call to accountability for a given local church is the pastor. The church members will be accountable as well, but on a lower level than the pastor.

Hebrews 13:17 is the clearest biblical passage on what it means to behave like sheep: "Obey those who rule over you, and be submissive, for they watch out for your souls, as those who must give account. Let them do so with joy and not with grief, for that would be unprofitable for you" (NKJV). I am a seminary professor, and I have some visibility as a national church leader, but I am also a member of a local church, New Life Church of Colorado Springs, and I submit myself to my pastor, Ted Haggard, and I obey him. God forbid that I would ever do anything to cause him grief. As I understand the Bible, any layperson who causes his or her pastor grief is out of the will of God! In my church, I am a sheep, and I try to behave like one.

3. Pay the money. Church growth costs money, and this money ultimately comes from the congregation. If you want your church to break the 200 barrier, you will do your share to provide the budget for it to happen. Americans are known as generous people, so one of the most surprising things to me is that church members only average about 3 percent of their income in giving to their churches. I am one of those who takes the Bible seriously when it says that if you do not give at least 10 percent of your income to the church, you are robbing God (see Mal. 3:8). My church has few money problems because we are taught to give.

4. Do the work of the ministry. Pastors are mentioned in Ephesians 4:11 as among those who have been assigned to equip "the saints for the work of ministry" (Eph. 4:12 NKJV) . The best way to do this is to help everyone in the congregation discover, develop, and use his or her spiritual gift or gifts. It is the responsibility of the pastor to see that this is done, but you must be willing to participate and carry your weight in doing the ministry of the church once you discover your gifts.

A crucial trade-off must take place if the church is to grow and break the 200 barrier. Lay people will have to give up their leadership for ministry, and the pastor will have to give up ministry for leadership. I realize that many will view this as a radical suggestion, but it is no more radical than, say, a heart bypass. If your physician suggests that a bypass might add ten years to your life, you would probably consider it. I am taking the role of a church doctor and suggesting that this trade-off could potentially add many more souls to the kingdom of God.

5. Accept newcomers. One of the major growth-obstructing diseases for any church, no matter what the size, is called "koinonitis." I have a whole chapter on it in my book *Your Church Can Be Healthy. Koinonia* is the Greek word for fellowship, and fellowship is one of the most positive characteristics of a local church. But in some churches, people enjoy their fellowship so much that it becomes the exclusive focus of their attention and participation in the life of the church. When this happens, the church suffers from "fellowship inflammation," which is not a blessing, but a disease. People become so focused on one another that they lose any vision they might have had for reaching the lost of their community. Koinonitis causes evangelistic myopia.

Furthermore, when new people visit a church with koinonitis they soon feel unwanted and unneeded. The sign outside might say "Visitors Welcome," but they do not find a welcome spirit on the inside. Unless koinonitis is cured, the church has little hope of ever seeing the other side of the 200 barrier.

6. Develop new fellowship circles. As I explained in the last chapter, Carl Dudley says that a small church is a single-cell church. Churches over the 200 barrier are multicelled churches. The transition from a single cell to many cells is usually extremely difficult because many will see it as a threat to the most essential quality of small churches, intimacy.

In a small church the congregation is one fellowship group. But the dynamics of a fellowship group begin to come apart when it approaches 80. Concrete steps must be taken to create a system in which church members, especially newcomers, can choose between several options for their fellowship groups. The larger the church becomes, the less the worship service is a fellowship group. Small groups must be formed for that purpose. These can be adult Sunday School classes, home cell groups, ministry teams, task-oriented groups, special interest groups, and many others. Many resources are available to pastors who desire to move from single cell to multicell, but the people must be willing to sacrifice a bit of the intimacy that they now enjoy as a part of the price to pay for breaking the 200 barrier.

You Can Do It!

Many things I have said in this chapter are difficult, but none of them is impossible. Remember: desire + commitment = motivation. If your church is not suffering from a terminal illness, you can grow and pass the 200 barrier if you want to grow enough to pay the price for growth. Just suppose that your church begins to grow and that ten years from now, as a result, there are 100 or 200 or 300 fewer people in hell than there otherwise would have been. How much would that be worth?

CHAPTER THREE

Action Steps toward Breaking the 200 Barrier

After having read what amounts to a full disclosure, if your church is willing to pay the price for growth, now is as good a time as any to begin to move toward breaking the 200 barrier. As I have said, I have no tried-and-true formula with a guarantee that any church that applies it will make it past 200. But I do have some good suggestions that have helped many a church move from a small church to a middle-sized church.

Get Ready . . . Prayer

Jesus said, "I will build my church" (Matt. 16:18). Although humans play key roles, church growth is not a human enterprise; it is a divine initiative. When all is said and done, God is the one who gives the increase and adds to the church. And nothing moves the hand of God like prayer. I like the way Jack Hayford puts it in his book, *Prayer Is Invading the Impossible:* "If we don't, He won't."[1] We don't know why an omnipotent God would so arrange the universe that some of the things he does are triggered by the prayers of mere mortals. But we do know that this is a fact. Therefore, let's not begin to move toward the 200 barrier without a solid foundation of prayer.

When we pray, it is good to know we are praying according to the will of God. Since God is not willing that any should perish (see 2 Pet. 3:9), we are sure that praying for the salvation of 100 or 200 people in our community through the ministry of our church is right on track. Here are some suggestions for upscaled prayer:

1. Pray for a filling of the Holy Spirit and a release of spiritual power in the congregation. Jesus said, "You shall receive power when the Holy Spirit has come upon you; and you shall be witnesses to Me" (Acts 1:8 NKJV).

2. Pray for divine wisdom. Important decisions for the future of the church need to be made. Which of these steps should we take first? What kind of a time line must we set? How do I communicate with my people so that they become motivated for growth? James wrote, "If any of you lacks wisdom, let him ask of God, who gives to all liberally and without re-proach, and it will be given to him" (Jas. 1:5 NKJV).

3. Pray for the fruit of the Spirit. If you read the last chapter, you know that a good bit of emotion will be involved in some of the changes that need to be made in order to break the 200 barrier. When this emotion surfaces, everyone involved will need an increase of love, longsuffering, kindness, goodness, and gentleness (see Gal. 5:22–23 NKJV). God wants to pro-vide this.

4. Pray for the gifts of the Spirit. Mobilizing the whole congre-gation for ministry must be based on discovering, developing,

and using the gifts of the Holy Spirit. If mobilization takes place in such a way, breaking the 200 barrier will not require much time.

5. Pray for evangelistic fruit. Chances are that the harvest in your town or city or neighborhood is more plentiful than you might think, and God is desiring to send out laborers into the harvest field (see Matt. 9:37–38). Pray that he will show you how to reach out effectively and that he will prepare divine appointments with unbelievers. Pray that your church will tool to meet the needs of new converts.

6. Pray that you will set the right goals. Each goal you set will give you a specific prayer target, and experience shows that targeted prayer is much more powerful than generalized prayer. Let's talk about setting goals.

Get Set . . . Goals

Every goal is a statement of faith, and the Bible teaches that "without faith it is impossible to please Him" (Heb. 11:6 NKJV). That is why setting goals has built-in spiritual power. Something happens when you set goals that would not happen without them. For example, David Yonggi Cho, a foremost advocate of prayer for growth and pastor of the world's largest church, makes this notable statement in one of his books: "The number one requirement for having real church growth—unlimited church growth— is to set goals."[2]

Here are the five characteristics of good goals:

1. Good goals are relevant. Be sure to set the right goals. If you break the 200 barrier, many new people will be coming into your church. Some will be transfers from other churches, but you need to set a goal for a good percentage of them to be new converts. Also do as good a job of diagnosing the health of your church as possible, and base your goals on accurate research.

2. Good goals are measurable. Avoid setting vague goals that you cannot measure. It is important to have a measuring instrument on hand for continuing assessment. You will also need a time frame for each goal. Such-and-such a thing by such-and-such a time. And be sure you have a system of accountability built in. If you announce your goal to your congregation, you have, ipso facto, adequate accountability. There are always people in your congregation who will hold your feet to the fire.

3. Good goals are significant. Each goal should make a substantial difference. Since setting goals involves faith, make sure your faith is big enough. Faith is the spiritual equivalent of muscle tissue—the more you use it, the stronger it gets. Body builders say, "No pain, no gain." Set goals that constantly stretch your faith.

4. Good goals are manageable. This goal balances the third one. Do not allow your goals to become so extravagant that you have no hope of accomplishing them. Stretch, but keep your goals within the range of possibility.

5. Good goals are personal. I once heard Ed Dayton say, "Do you want to know the difference between good goals and bad goals? Good goals are my goals and bad goals are your goals!" When you think of it, this statement is true. Therefore, when you are casting the vision for your congregation you must do it in such a way as to achieve goal ownership on the part of the opinion makers and influencers among them.

Go . . . Breaking the Barrier

As I begin to give some concrete suggestions for breaking the 200 barrier, I will first take the easiest way—to start a new church, and never stop at the 200 barrier. Back when I was first preparing this lesson for my classes at Fuller Seminary, my wife, Doris, was talking on the telephone to Bill Sullivan, founder of the Church

Growth Department of the Church of the Nazarene, and she said, "Peter is working on breaking the 200 barrier. How do you do it?" Bill replied in one word: "Quickly!"

What was Bill Sullivan saying? He was saying that the new church should never be a small church. Remember Carl Dudley's statement? "Small is something more than a numerical description." Even though the new church may have only 50 or 100 members, it does not need to be a small church or have a small church mindset. For starters, it must never allow itself to be a single cell.

I instruct my church planters to plan on breaking the 200 barrier the first year. If they do not break it the second year, the probability of ever breaking it decreases very rapidly. But, if they do a good enough job on site selection in order to trigger positive contextual factors, any church with adequate leadership should be able to do it in two years. I then give them a checklist of six items to begin implementing from day one so that they will never stop at the 200 barrier.

Obviously, the great majority of those reading this book do not have the luxury of planting a brand new church. Turning a long-established church around is a much more formidable challenge. I will make some specific observations on that situation a bit later. Meanwhile, I will offer important growth principles through the following points that you will absolutely have to keep in mind if you hope to turn your older church around.

Six Ways to Avoid Stopping at the 200 Barrier

1. Staffing

I tell my church planters to begin their new churches with two staff members instead of one. By this I mean *program* staff, not *support* staff such as office workers. Staff members do not have to work full time at first, but they should move toward full time as soon as possible. I realize that for some this option is impossible and that the only option is to start with one staff member, the pastor. If that is the case, plans should be made to add the second staff person before reaching 100 active adults and the third before reaching 200, continuing this ratio until the church reaches 500. Then it is time for reassessment.

Many will say that this suggestion for staffing sounds like too much. The reason for this attitude is that the existing models we have for church staff are *maintenance* models, not *growth* models. Most churches under the 200 barrier are adequately staffed for maintenance, but not for growth. Adding staff to an existing church won't cause that church to start growing, but when the growth process begins you will need more staff than you have now.

When you add staff, whom do you add? My advice is not to add a position but to add a person. The person you add should fit three criteria: (1) he agrees with and fits your church's philosophy of ministry; (2) he brings spiritual gifts to the staff that supplement existing gifts; and (3) he exhibits total loyalty to the senior pastor.

2. Fellowship groups

Here is the principle: start the new church with *multiple options for adult fellowship groups*. Why is this so important? Because if you succeed in doing it properly, your church will never be a single-cell church, which is one of the most difficult things to change once it develops.

To give an example, my friend Rick Warren, author of *The Purpose Driven Church*, knew these principles as well as anyone when he planted Saddleback Community Church back in 1980. In those days we met together frequently. When he had reached 150 members, I remember reminding him that he was now at the most crucial growth point his church would ever encounter. He knew it very well, but even so, he stalled out at the 200 barrier for a couple of years. This put him under so much stress that he had to take a four-month sabbatical in the California desert to recuperate. He is now just fine, and the church is well over 10,000 and on its way to his original goal of 20,000. I mention this situation here because, even though he tried to keep it from happening, Rick Warren found his church exhibiting the characteristics of a single-cell church.

If you begin your new church as a cell-based church, which many are doing these days, you have a built-in design to avoid becoming a single-cell church. If you do not choose to do so, you will have to take other steps to avoid becoming a single-cell church. Remember, it will not happen by itself. It is natural for a church to be single-celled. This is part of pumping that water uphill.

3. Leadership mode

Start your church as an *equipper*, not as an *enabler*. In my book *Leading Your Church to Growth*, I elaborate on this a great deal, and I define an equipper as follows: "An equipper is a leader who actively sets goals for a congregation according to the will of God, obtains goal ownership from the people, and sees that each church member is properly motivated and equipped to do his or her part in accomplishing the goals."[3]

Everyone who comes into the new church should clearly understand that the pastor does the leading and the people do the ministry. In the majority of older churches, however, this crucial growth principle is totally out of kilter.

4. Pastoral function

Start the church as a *rancher*, not as a *shepherd*. I explained this in some detail in the last chapter. It is hard for some to picture how they can start a brand new church and not shepherd all the people, but they can, as long as there is mutual agreement that this is the way it is done in our church. This mutual agreement requires three basic ingredients: (1) the pastor does not visit the hospital, (2) the pastor does not call on church members in their homes, and (3) the pastor does no personal counseling.

This list will come as a shock to many members of older churches because they feel that this is exactly what they hire the pastor to do. The question for them then becomes: How deeply are you really committed to breaking the 200 barrier?

5. Facilities

It is best to start the new church in leased or rented facilities. A church often starts in a private home, often the pastor's home. When it outgrows the living room or the family room, it moves to a strip mall or a hotel conference room or a school or a warehouse or any place with enough room in a reasonable location. Stay in such facilities as long as possible, at least until you are well past the 200 barrier, say at about 350 active members. Rick Warren used 40 or 50 different rented facilities until Saddleback Community Church reached about 6,000. Then they built and moved into permanent facilities.

I think that the one most avoidable decision that has kept churches under the 200 barrier is building a church building too soon. Many who are reading this book will identify with that because they are currently located in one of those buildings. Here is a thought that might work in some instances. Sell the present facility, and deposit the money in a trust fund earmarked for future building. Then begin to use rented facilities like many new churches do, and follow their pattern. It might also be a suitable occasion to change the name of the church if a more attractive name might be available.

6. Bylaws

I tell my church planters to try to avoid writing bylaws for the church until they have 500 members. The reason for this is that most traditional models of bylaws, reflecting American democracy, are designed to siphon off authority from the pastor and deposit it in the congregation. An unwritten rule in traditional churches is that you can trust groups but you cannot trust individuals very much.

Challenges for Existing Churches

It is much more difficult to get the church off a plateau than never to stop at one. It is also much more difficult to break the single-cell syndrome than never to allow one to develop. That is why so many churches under 200 will remain under 200 forever. But it is not impossible to turn things around. For example, Jack Hayford came into what is now Church on the Way in Van Nuys, California, when the church had long been plateaued under 100. Under his leadership it broke the 200 barrier and is now around 7,500.

To be as realistic as possible about the existing church, breaking the 200 barrier is a special challenge if:

1. The church is plateaued or declining.

2. The church is ten years old or older.

3. The current pastor has been there 6 years or longer.

4. The church building lacks visibility and accessibility.

5. Kinship ties form a significant part of the social network of the congregation.

6. The congregation has considerably more members in their 50s than in their 30s.

Breaking the 200 barrier is more likely to happen if all, or at least several, of these characteristics are present in the existing church:

1. The church has a relatively new pastor with a mutual expectation of at least five years tenure.

2. The pastor has the ability to identify the formal and informal lay leadership structures and locate the power centers.

3. The pastor has the patience and wisdom to spend substantial personal time to build relationships with the opinion-makers and permission-granters.

4. The pastor has the courage to withstand the threat of long-term members of the church leaving under protest.

5. The church is willing to begin thinking like a large church.

Thinking Like a Large Church

Many of today's large churches have never been small churches. Remember that Carl Dudley says that small is something more than a numerical description. Such churches went through a period of time when they had only a few members, but they were never small churches because they never allowed the small church mind-set to make inroads. The effect of small numbers was neutralized by a positive mind-set and a commitment to growth goals strong enough to pay any price necessary.

In recent years, and more than ever before, a considerable number of megachurches has surfaced here in America. Several researchers have studied these churches in order to discover their common characteristics. If churches under the 200 barrier are serious about growth, they would do well to emulate as many of these characteristics as possible.

1. Conservative theology. These churches are, by and large, evangelical churches. They hold a high view of biblical authority, and they are convinced that an individual's personal relationship to Jesus Christ makes the difference between heaven and hell. Because of this, evangelism is a top priority in these churches. In his excellent book, *Church for the Unchurched* (Abingdon Press), George Hunter calls them "apostolic congregations," implying that aggressive outreach is in their DNA.

2. Strong pastoral leadership. A rule of church growth is that the larger the church the more crucial the role of the senior pastor. In most small churches, that role is far from crucial. Pastors come and go every three or four years, and the

church goes on like the Energizer bunny. Small churches that hope to break the 200 barrier will have to change this understanding of the pastor's role. In larger churches the authority of the pastor is unquestioned, and thoughts of the pastor ever leaving are not entertained. The pastor casts an optimistic vision for the future, he persuades the people that they have received this vision from God, and he motivates his people for action.

3. Participatory worship. Most of these new large churches have an aversion to performance in worship. They give a low profile to robed choirs and pipe organs. Their worship is long, with up to 35 or 45 minutes of singing, mostly without hymnals and with the words of the songs projected on the wall or on screens. Many of the songs they sing were written within the past few years or even the past months. The worship style offers considerable freedom for body language, with some people standing, others sitting, others kneeling, some with hands up, and a good bit of clapping. Much more than in standard-brand churches, the congregation feels like it is directly participating in worship and helping to make it happen.

4. Powerful prayer. Prayer is high profile and up front in most of these congregations. They have a high level of congregational participation in the prayer life and ministry of the church because the people strongly believe that prayer will actually change things. A few of these churches have a staff person whose ministry is dedicated to prayer: "pastor of intercession" or words to that effect.

5. The centrality of the Holy Spirit. The Holy Spirit is often featured as a prominent member of the Trinity in contrast to other churches, which tend to give the third person of the Trinity a subordinate role in church life. Some traditional churches almost feel embarrassment if the Holy Spirit is mentioned too much, but not these newer, dynamic churches. Both the

person and the work of the Holy Spirit are cultivated in church life.

6. Abundant finances. These large churches are not immune to financial crises from time to time, but as a rule, money is no problem. Whether people should tithe their income to the church is not a subject of debate. Tithing is more often seen as a declaration of commitment to Christ and to the body of Christ. When believers tithe, even seemingly extravagant church budgets are met.

7. Lay ministry. Each church member is expected to carry his or her weight in carrying out the ministry of the church. Teaching on spiritual gifts is prominent, and application is facilitated. Some of these churches have developed in-house training programs akin to a Bible institute. Churches that offer these training programs will simultaneously set in place an open track from the congregation to the church staff, including ordination.

8. Practical Bible teaching. These churches offer extensive Bible teaching, but with an important twist. Rather than beginning sermon preparation with an exegesis of a Scripture text, most of these megachurch pastors begin with an exegesis of their congregation and choose Scripture that promises to heal their hurts and meet their needs. Sermons are very down-to-earth and practical, with immediate applications.

9. Direct missions involvement. Many of these large congregations recruit, train, and send their own missionaries, bypassing traditional mission agencies. Short-term mission trips, frequently led by the pastor, are common. A higher and higher percentage of church members are themselves being exposed to overseas mission-field situations, and the changes that come into their lives through such experiences tend to permeate the whole congregation, raising the level of missions consciousness.

10. Low denominational profile. When these newer mega-churches take root within traditional denominational structures, they and their pastors are frequently an embarrassment to officials in the denominational headquarters and an implicit threat to pastors of smaller churches in the denomination. Some of them even take generic names for their local churches, either dropping the denominational designation or relegating it to fine print.

Conclusion

Breaking the 200 barrier is the most widespread growth challenge for churches across America and around the world. Few churches mired in smallness and lethargy even know that a 200 barrier exists. Some of the better informed ones suspect its existence, but they understand little or nothing about how to go about breaking it. Yet others do know what it takes to break the 200 barrier but are unwilling to pay the price. My prayer is that more and more churches will break out of this status quo syndrome, get under the burden for reaching the unchurched in their communities, bring them to Christ, nurture them in their congregations, and participate directly in the exciting enterprise of extending the kingdom of God!

PART 2

OVERCOMING MIDDLE-SIZED CHURCH

GROWTH BARRIERS OF 400 PEOPLE

BY

THOM S. RAINER

Thom S. Rainer, born in 1955, is the founding dean of the Billy Graham School of Missions, Evangelism and Church Growth at the Southern Baptist Theological Seminary in Louisville, Kentucky. His Ph.D. dissertation from the seminary is considered one of the most significant research projects about the Church Growth Movement: "An Assessment of C. Peter Wagner's Contributions to the Theology of Church Growth."

Thom Rainer came to the Southern Baptist Theological Seminary as dean of the Billy Graham School after serving as senior pastor of four growing churches. The last church he served grew to nearly 2,000 in membership during his tenure there.

Since Rainer became dean of the school, several degree programs have been established: the Master of Divinity, the Master of Theology, the Doctor of Missiology, the Doctor of Ministry, and the Doctor of Philosophy, all in specific areas of Great Commission Studies. The Graham School has become one of the fastest growing and most reputable schools in its field. Elmer Towns and Peter Wagner think Thom is one of the brightest new lights on the church growth horizon.

Rainer is married to the former Nellie Jo King. They have three sons: Sam, Art, and Jess.

CHAPTER FOUR

Barriers to Growth in
the
Middle-Sized Church

Two churches. Similar neighborhoods in the same section of a small metropolitan area of 100,000 people. Budgets are virtually identical, and the demographics of their communities are amazingly similar. Neither church had indebtedness in 1993. Both had well-kept buildings that could handle 300 in worship and a like number for Sunday School.

In 1993 Forest Springs Community Church had an attendance of 220, and Eastern Valley Church counted 195 each week. Five years later Forest Springs Community Church's attendance had declined to 205 while Eastern Valley Church had doubled to 390.

The brief stories of these two churches are true. The names are fictitious, but the facts are accurate. Within just five years one church had doubled while the other had declined slightly. Yet, on the surface, the two churches were amazingly similar in 1993. How could each of the churches be so different just five years later?

The Middle-Sized Church Enigma

The story of Forest Springs Community Church and Eastern Valley Church presents us first a question: What is a middle-sized church? In the above account, both churches had an attendance of approximately 200 in 1993. Is it then accurate to say that the 200-attendance church is middle-sized?

Lyle Schaller would say that both Forest Springs Community Church and Eastern Valley Church are as close to the category of the large church as they are to the middle-sized church.[1] Statistically, his point is well made. Approximately one third of the people who attend a Protestant worship service this Sunday will be in churches with an attendance of less than 100. Slightly over 30 percent will be in churches with an average attendance between 100 and 200. Another 38 percent will be in churches that average more than 200.[2]

By statistical norms then, both Forest Springs Community Church and Eastern Valley Church were in the upper range of middle-sized churches in 1993. By 1998, however, Eastern Valley was clearly a large church by numerical standards. Its attendance of 390 would place it in the upper 20 percent of churches in America.

Having worked with hundreds of churches across our nation, I realize that neat statistical categories do not always best describe churches. I therefore will define the middle-sized church as one whose culture is neither that of the small church nor the large church. I realize that this definition is a bit nebulous, so I will elaborate further.

If you have already read Peter Wagner's section in this book, you realize that small churches have a certain culture or mentality.

The people respond as if the church is a single-cell or single-family unit. Everyone knows everyone else. Though formal meetings may be held, most decisions are made by a patriarch, a matriarch, or a small power group.

Elmer Towns will later describe large churches, those churches with an attendance approaching or exceeding 1,000 in number. These churches are obviously not single family or single cell, but neither are they single congregations. Their culture is more like several churches or several cultures held together by common beliefs, worship styles, location, or leaders.

But the middle-sized church responds as neither a single cell on the small end nor the multiple congregation on the large end. This category of churches is so expansive and so diverse that Schaller concludes "about all they have in common is their size."[3] He is right. Sometimes the middle-sized church is best defined by what it is not.

I am the father of three teenage sons. As of this writing, my boys are ages 18, 16, and 13. My older two sons, Sam and Art, often display adult tendencies, but they have not matured to the point where their behavior and attitude are always like that of an adult. My youngest son, Jess, is still a kid at heart. But as he breaks into the ranks of adolescence, I see him abandoning some of the childlike tendencies he had just last year.

The maturity level of my boys, it seems, can best be described by what it is not. The boys are neither young children nor are they adults. And even though there is a significant difference between the maturity level of my oldest and my youngest, they share some common characteristics.

So it is with the middle-sized churches. Some of the churches have a culture that often acts like a small church. Others behave more like large churches. But neither group responds exclusively like the large or small churches.

Middle-sized churches are difficult to define. Even more difficult is the task of identifying the growth barriers that apply specifically to this category of churches. Though the task is difficult, it is not impossible. Later in this chapter we will examine these barriers. In the next chapter we will look at ways to overcome the barriers.

Before we look at the issue of barriers, we need to examine biblical issues that may be especially pertinent to the middle-sized church. What does the Bible say about the middle-sized church?

Biblical Issues for the Middle-Sized Church

The Bible never specifically addresses churches in regard to size or attendance level. When the writers of Scripture were inspired by the Holy Spirit (see 2 Tim. 3:16) to address churches, the letters concerned foundational, doctrinal, behavioral, and polity issues.

For the church at Rome and the churches of Galatia, the concern was the very nature of the gospel. For the church at Corinth the issues were church unity and Christian behavior. For the church at Ephesus the letter addressed the necessity of Christlike living. For the Philippian church, a primary issue was joy in adversity. Paul wrote to the Colossian church because of his concern about heretical teaching. To the Thessalonian church the issue of the return of Christ was explored. And to Timothy and Titus, church leaders, Paul addressed matters of polity and doctrine.

In all of these churches, plus the seven churches in Revelation, the Bible does not specifically address issues concerning size. What we discover, however, is that failure to grow or to overcome growth barriers is often *symptomatic* of disobedience to biblical truths. Let us explore a few such examples.

The Great Commission
Almost every book dealing with the biblical basis of evangelism and church growth cites the Great Commission as one of the most significant mandates in Scripture. The text in Matthew is the most-often cited: "Go therefore and make disciples of all the

nations, baptizing them in the name of the Father and the Son and the Holy Spirit, teaching them to observe all that I commanded you; and lo, I am with you always, even to the end of the age" (28:19–20 NASB).

The words of Christ set the priority that the church followed after his ascension. The mandate is to "go." The focus of the church was to look beyond itself. In an earlier work, I called this perspective the "outward focus" mandate.[4]

What is amazing but no longer surprising is that so many churches only give lip service to the Great Commission. Negligible resources of time, people, and money are dedicated to the task of "going." I recently visited a church with an average attendance of 400 and a budget of $425,000. The Great Commission was visible on all of this church's newsletters and bulletins. But upon further examination, I discovered that the church had no intentional plan to reach its community; it had nominal dollars in the budget for outreach, and only six people were reached for Christ in the past year.

As we will see further in this chapter, the middle-sized church can be a comfortable size for many people. The church is sufficiently large for multiple programs, but it is not so large that one feels unimportant or unneeded. Many members thus feel that "we are just the right size," so the motivation to reach others is diminished. The problem is, this mind-set is sinful disobedience to the Great Commission and cannot be ignored.

The Great Commandment

When a scribe asked Jesus, "'What commandment is the foremost of all?'" (Mark 12:28 NASB), Jesus answered: "'And you shall love the Lord your God with all your heart, and with all your soul, and with all your mind, and with all your strength. The second is this, You shall love your neighbor as yourself. There is no other commandment greater than these'" (Mark 12:30–31 NASB).

The second portion of the Great Commandment is to love persons other than ourselves. While this commandment was addressed to individual believers, it has a corporate application in the local church. The comfort factor mentioned in reference to the Great Commission can likewise engender disobedience to the Great Commandment. When the church's comfort is of greater concern than reaching out to others in love, it has reached both spiritual and numerical barriers.

The Ephesians Four Factor

The apostle Paul was deeply concerned about the unity and the building up of the church, the body of Christ. He thus spoke of the church with its "proper working of each individual part, [which] causes the growth of the body for the building up of itself in love" (Eph. 4:16 NASB).

How did Paul view the church as growing best? In earlier verses in chapter 4, he cited the mandate that every person in the church should be doing ministry. The apostles, prophets, evangelists, and pastors/teachers were to equip members for ministry: "And He gave some as apostles, and some as prophets, and some as evangelists, and some as pastors and teachers, for the equipping of the saints for the work of service, to the building up of the body of Christ" (Eph. 4:11–12 NASB).

The mandate is clear. Everyone is to be involved in ministry. If all of the saints are not doing the work of service, the body of Christ, the church is not built. For many middle-sized churches, this issue is critical. They are unable to grow beyond a certain size because the bulk of ministry is done by the pastor or other paid staff. More on this barrier later.

The Acts 2 Fellowship Factor

The small church can refuse to grow beyond its one cell because of an unbiblical contentedness with its holy-huddle fellowship. The middle-sized church, though larger than a single-cell group, can also become unbiblically comfortable with its existing relationship and fellowship patterns.

In a recent study conducted by the Billy Graham School of Missions, Evangelism and Church Growth at The Southern Baptist Theological Seminary, several hundred laypersons were asked to name the purposes of the church. Less than one fourth responded that evangelism was a purpose of the church, but nearly 90 percent viewed fellowship as a key function.[5]

While one can support biblically the place of fellowship in the church, the laypersons' concept of evangelizing the world in this research project was disconcerting. For the majority, fellowship was "taking care of our people" or "loving our people in our church." Repeatedly the emphasis was on "our people" and "our church."

Certainly the concept of *koinonia* or "fellowship" refers to the church persons: "They were continually devoting themselves to the apostles' teaching and to *fellowship*" (Acts 2:42 NASB, emphasis added). But that fellowship among the believers made certain that their ministry extended into the unchurched community. As a consequence, "the Lord was adding to their number day by day those who were being saved" (Acts 2:47 NASB).

St. John's Syndrome

Peter Wagner, in his excellent book, *The Healthy Church*, describes the church "disease" he calls St. John's Syndrome.[6] The name is derived from the human author of the Revelation, the apostle John. The apostle wrote letters to seven churches, among them the church at Laodicea. To this body he wrote on behalf of Christ: "'I know your deeds, that you are neither cold nor hot; I wish that you were cold or hot. So because you are lukewarm, and neither hot nor cold, I will spit you out of My mouth'" (Rev. 3:15–16 NASB).

The fellowships in many churches are no longer vibrant and outward-focused bodies. Their churches are mere organizations. Their passion for reaching the lost has waned or died. Their hunger for prayer and God's Word is no longer evident. These churches are not Great Commission churches, but social clubs.

When you observe members, particularly leaders, in these churches, you discover that they get more excited about bylaws than winning souls to Christ. They will cause an unholy uproar if Robert's Rules of Order are violated, but they will not even whimper if the Bible is ignored. They are more concerned about their pew, their classroom, or how fifty dollars was spent rather than the realization that over half of their community is hell-bound without Christ.

Though middle-sized churches do not alone contract St. John's Syndrome, they do seem more susceptible to the disease than other churches. Again, the comfort factor often explains their lukewarmness. They may have no crises of money and programs. They are sufficiently large to meet the needs of their own but unmotivated to meet the needs of others.

Two years ago I consulted a church that clearly was infected with the disease of St. John's Syndrome. Fortunately, a few persons in the church realized their malady. For eighteen months this handful of people met regularly, repented of the church's sin of lukewarmness, and prayed that God's Spirit would revive the congregation.

God answered the prayers of those faithful few, and a true revival touched the church. Unfortunately, over fifty people resisted the work of God and eventually left the church. But that loss of fifty was more than compensated by the growth that revival brought. To this day that middle-sized church continues to grow. Soon it will enter the ranks of the large-sized churches.

I often use that church as a model to explain the strengths of the middle-sized church. Exactly what advantages are inherent in churches of this size?

The Strengths of the Middle-Sized Church

No two middle-sized churches are alike. It is therefore presumptuous to identify all such churches with common characteristics.

However, in two recent studies involving nearly one thousand churches, I did discover some common traits of middle-sized churches that could be called strengths.[7]

Beyond the Single-Cell Church

Perhaps the greatest single strength of the middle-sized church is that it is no longer constrained to the limitations of the small, single-cell church. A church I visited in the Atlanta metropolitan area provides a good example of this strength.

The church was an independent congregation with an attendance of fewer than 100 in the early 1980s. The community in which it was located was considered small town with a number of persons from nearby rural areas.

The growth of metropolitan Atlanta in the eighties and early nineties affected the small town profoundly. Many Atlanta workers began to move to the area as the community transitioned from small town to a growing bedroom community.

The church did not experience any of the growth affecting the community initially. Several factors hindered the growth of the church. First, the financial resources of the church were so limited that only bills of absolute necessity could be paid. No funds were available to reach out to the new residents or to offer attractive programs.

Second, all decisions were made by an elderly husband and wife. The woman's family had been in control of the church for a century, although she was the lone survivor of the family still in the church.

Finally, the church facilities were in terrible condition. The church seemed in an unlikely position to grow beyond its small-church status. But three significant developments quickly changed this scenario.

First, the pastor retired and moved to Florida. Second, the elderly couple, the "power center," died within a few months of each other. Third, a small group of people began to pray that God would send a pastor to lead them beyond their present woeful state. This group of four to seven persons met twice a week early in the morning to pray for the prospective pastor and for a true spiritual awakening.

God heard and answered the prayers. A thirty-six-year-old pastor sensed the call of God to the small church, despite numerous offers from other congregations. The people followed his leadership and began to do the work of ministry with him. Growth came slowly initially, but it was steady growth.

As the congregation grew, though still at an incremental pace, funds became available for programs and ministries beyond basic financial survival. A building renovation fund was established, and the old building began to change dramatically.

As more new residents moved into the area, many heard about the small church that was reaching out to the community. Visitors were impressed with the efforts to make the facilities attractive, useful, safe, and clean. More growth took place, and more funds became available for further ministry and renovation of the facilities.

By 1990 the church averaged more than 300 in attendance. In 1997 the average attendance was 550. Now the church has greater resources to reach out to an even greater extent. Indeed its strengths include all of those in the following sections.

Expanded Financial and Ministry Resources

Many small churches find themselves in a "catch-22." They desire to grow, but they do not have the resources to grow. And the only way they can get additional resources is by growing.

By contrast, many middle-sized churches do have expanded resources. They are not constrained with the dilemma of paying only the bills necessary for survival. Because of their expanded financial resources, some of these middle-sized churches are able to offer more ministries and programs, which can help engender numerical growth. They have many more options than the small single-cell churches.

When I mention the blessings of expanded resources of the middle-sized churches in conferences, I am inevitably confronted by someone who vociferously disagrees. "You don't understand our church," the pastor might say. "We desperately need another full-time minister, and our secretary needs to be full-time as well. I simply don't agree that we have expanded resources."

Yet, when I begin to question the pastor about the church's programs, ministry, and personnel, I discover that the church is more blessed than he realizes. It is natural that the leadership would desire more staff and other resources, but the church is doing far more than many small churches whose mission is often survival.

Indeed the issue with the middle-sized church is often the allocation of resources rather than survival. Schaller often calls the middle-sized church the "awkward-sized church" because it is the "type of congregation [in which] the wants and needs often exceed the resources."[8]

Expanded Leadership

I pastored Hopewell Baptist Church in Jeffersontown, Kentucky, early in my ministry. Jeffersontown was a small community with a rural flavor. Change has come to the town rather dramatically in the past two decades as the Louisville metropolitan area has grown toward Jeffersontown. Now the community is considered a suburb of Louisville.

The church had an average attendance of about 80 when I began my ministry there. Because I was a full-time doctoral student at seminary, I was limited in the amount of time I could give the church.

Out of desperation, I began to ask laypersons to assume roles that had been normally expected of the pastor. Evangelistic outreach, ministry to the homebound, Sunday School leadership, and a plethora of other ministry roles were led by laypersons. Because of their involvement, the church began to grow significantly. Within eighteen months our attendance grew to 130 as we reached the new residents of our area.

God blessed that church as it made the transition from small to middle-sized. One of the most significant changes involved the people's expectations of the pastor. The people realized that ministry was not the sole domain of one person. The leadership and ministry base had expanded.

Most pastors in middle-sized churches are blessed because they are not expected to carry the full load of ministry in the church. Indeed the church could not have grown to its size without expanding its ministry and leadership base.

Again, I am often challenged when I make this observation. So many pastors are working unbelievably long hours because so much work needs to be done. They find it painfully amusing when I speak about the blessings of expanded leadership in the middle-sized church.

But when their ministry is compared to the ministry of pastors in small churches, the blessings become more apparent. To illustrate, a pastor of a 30-member church recently responded to a pastor of a middle-sized church in one of my conferences: "Yesterday I typed the bulletin, cleaned the church bathroom, opened and responded to all the mail, ordered Sunday School literature, repaired a leak in the roof, and took out the trash from last Sunday. I wish I had time to do the ministry you're complaining about."

Indeed most ministry situations are less than ideal in the middle-sized church. But, if one honestly evaluates the scenario, it is much better than in those churches where only one or a very few do everything.

The Loyalty Factor

A recent study I led on assimilation opened my eyes to the intense loyalty present in many middle-sized congregations.[9] Such loyalty was present in the small churches, but it was typically limited to just a few people. In the larger churches, the loyalty factor was not nearly as pervasive.

Listen to the comments of a member of a 275-attendance church: "When I was a member of [a church with an attendance of 60], all the decisions were made by one family and their closest friends. I never had a say in anything. At this church I am able to choose from several programs and ministries without worrying if a few people will mess up things."[10]

While the members of larger churches indicated some degree of loyalty, their dedication typically was not as intense as that of the participants in middle-sized churches. "Belonging" was a word often used to describe the experience of the middle-sized church participants in contrast to the members of the large churches. The church was not so large that members felt as if they were not needed or wanted. But the church was not so small that they sensed that all decision-making authority resided in a few people.

In our study on assimilation of nearly 300 churches, we asked the following question in follow-up interviews of laypersons: "On a scale of one to ten, with ten being the highest, how would you rate your sense of loyalty to the church of which you are a member?"[11]

The results confirmed that members of middle-sized churches tend to be more loyal than members of small or large churches. They are more willing to stay with the church in difficult times. Our research indicates that this loyalty factor increases up to an average attendance of 399, at which point it begins to decline.

This pattern of loyalty has significant implications for the leadership of the middle-sized churches. It means that pastors can count on a large portion of their membership to "weather the storms." It means that assimilation can be more effective. And it means that barriers to growth can be broken. Indeed, those barriers are the focus of this book and this chapter. Let us look at several of the barriers in the second half of this chapter. In the following chapter we will look at possible ways to overcome the barriers.

Growth Barriers in the Middle-Sized Church

As I began this chapter, I tried to make it very clear that definitions are difficult for the middle-sized church. Peter Wagner articulated definitions of churches of different sizes established by

Lyle Schaller, William Tinsley, Douglas Walrath, Carl Dudley, and himself. Though they were similar, none were identical.

Even more difficult is the process of identifying barriers unique to the middle-sized church. At the Billy Graham School of Missions, Evangelism and Church Growth at Southern Seminary, however, we have been blessed with a wonderful research team. This team has gathered an abundance of data from churches across our nation. I think this information can help give us some keen insights into growth barriers.

We looked at data from 600 churches of varying locations and backgrounds. The attendance of the churches ranged from 200 to 500. About 400 of these churches were in statistical decline or plateau; the remaining 200 churches had broken growth barriers in recent years.

We were able to interview a good sampling of each of these groups of churches to determine differences between the growing churches and the nongrowing churches. In the remainder of this chapter, I will identify the top sixteen barriers to the middle-sized church. In the chapter which follows, we will look at ways to overcome these barriers.

The barriers noted in the following pages are not always mutually exclusive. Indeed in nongrowing middle-sized churches, it is rare that only one barrier would be present. Although I have listed each of the barriers in order of the frequency of occurrence, typically one church will have three to five obstacles clearly present.

Barrier #1: "Comfortitis"

The most common barrier we found in the nongrowing, middle-sized churches was comfort with the status quo. In our interviews with the members of these churches the following comments were typical:

- "We like our church just the way it is."

- "If we grow larger, we won't know everyone."

- "We can't grow anymore in our present sanctuary. And I sure don't want to have multiple worship services."

- "We've got just the right number of programs and ministries."

- "This church is the way I remember it when I was a kid. I hope it never changes."

- "You know, the attraction of the bar in 'Cheers' is that everybody knows your name. That's the way it is in our church."

As I will discuss in the next chapter, this barrier is one of the most difficult to overcome because most of the people in the church are happy. Indeed, growth will often move the majority of the church from contentedness to discontentedness. And what pastor is eager to move his congregation into conflict?

Barrier #2: Participatory Democracy

I am a Southern Baptist, a denomination that fiercely defends the autonomy of each local congregation. Indeed, each church is Southern Baptist by choice. Any local body can sever its ties with the denomination at its own bidding.

Within each local church, many members feel that everyone should have a part in participating in virtually every decision in the church. This concept of participatory democracy seems fair and "American," but it can bring the process of growth to a grinding halt.

I recently sat in on the monthly business meeting of a church with an average attendance of about 400. The major issue of the meeting was a recent personnel decision. As a consequence, numerous individuals wanted to offer their input on a job description, and consensus was never reached. Many left angry, feeling that their perspectives had not been considered. The fact of the matter is that many conflicting views were evident. There was no way everyone could be happy with the decision that was made.

The tragedy is that this issue dominated the life of the church for the next several weeks. Recent emphases on outreach and missions were overshadowed by the divisive business meeting.

Is it possible to be an autonomous church, yet function without the divisiveness and detractions that a participatory democracy can bring? The answer is "yes" with qualifications. We will examine this issue in the next chapter.

Barrier #3: The Power Group Syndrome

When our research revealed that the Power Group Syndrome was the third most frequently mentioned barrier to growth, I identified immediately. It is not unusual for a small cadre of people to control most of the decision making in a small church. This group may be a deacon board, family members, or an informal coalition of long-time members.

The reason I identified so readily was my own experience as a pastor. A recent seminary graduate, I was eager to move my church to new levels of numerical and spiritual growth. The growth came rather easily as we transitioned from a small church to a middle-sized church within two years. The problems came when we attempted to move past barriers as a middle-sized church.

The rather vocal opposition of my leadership and my staff's leadership came from a very small but very obvious power group within the church. They had been able to hold on to their power when the church was small and up to some levels that would be categorized as middle-sized. But their power base was severely threatened as growth continued.

They never articulated their loss of power as the "problem" with my leadership or the direction of the church (they rarely do). But they made every attempt to become a veto voice to any leadership moves that we attempted to make, especially those that might dilute their power base even more. How we and other church leaders overcame the barrier is discussed in the next chapter.

Barrier #4: The Not-Like-Us Malady

This barrier has similar characteristics to the Power Group Syndrome. The primary similarity is the perception that new members ("the outsiders") are changing the church from the way it used to be. In the case of the power group, the fear is the loss of power. In the case of the not-like-us malady, the fear is change itself. The church is different from the way the old guard remembers it. The newcomers are ruining the "good old days."

The threat becomes evident to the old guard as new members come into positions of influence and leadership in the church. When the old guard perceives that the newer members are about to have the power to make changes in the church, the conflict arises. When this malady is present, the old guard will resist any kind of effort that would yield church growth. The new members are seen as outsiders who are messing up the church they love.

Barrier #5: Ministry Misplacement

This barrier is the result of too few trying to do too much of the ministry. Perhaps the pastor, one staff person, and three or four key lay leaders are attempting to do the bulk of ministry in the church. They were able to bring the church from small to middle-sized. But now the church can grow no further. The few ministers, staff or lay, are stretched to their limits. The church has grown to its full potential unless new people are unleashed to do the work of ministry.

Barrier #6: The Pastoral Care Pastor

Church growth rarely occurs without pain or cost. Conversely, the personal attention and care a pastor can give to individual members typically results in responses of love and accolades. Which of the two responses would a pastor typically choose? Pain and conflict or love and accolades?

Many pastors have indeed chosen the path of pastoral care, which yields an abundance of affirmation. But such a choice typically means that the church will grow only to the point that the pastor can give some level of personal attention to all the active members. And that level of growth is usually met in the lower range of attendance in the middle-sized church.

Barrier #7: Biblical Blindness

I recently spoke at a conference where I casually mentioned that true kingdom growth through a local church is correlated to biblical fidelity. I further said that lasting church growth will not occur unless the people in the church have a high view of Scripture.

When I later read the evaluations of my conference, I received a scathing indictment of my comments. I was chastised for being "narrow-minded" and "insisting that people agree with my neat and tidy theological system." All I said was that we must believe the Bible!

When Dean Kelley wrote *Why Conservative Churches Are Growing* in 1972,[12] he received similar comments, many from his mainline peers. His thesis has been supported many times over. Church growth *is* related to a "strict" understanding of the Bible. My research on evangelistic churches in 1996 provided objective verification to the long-standing Kelley thesis.[13]

A church can grow to a certain point with programs, social ministries, and good organization. But long-standing conversion growth simply does not take place in churches that have a more liberal view of Scripture. Many liberal churches have found themselves at a middle-sized barrier due primarily to their beliefs about the Bible.

Although objective verification of the Kelley thesis has taken place several times, common sense can also lead to the same conclusion. How can a church have an evangelistic urgency without a "strict" view of the exclusivity of salvation through Christ, of the sinfulness and lostness of humanity, and of the literal reality of heaven and hell?

Barrier #8: Small Church Mentality

Some churches reach barriers because the members can never see their fellowship as anything but a small church. Ironically, many leaders in middle-sized churches are small-church minded. Their church may have overcome the 100 or 200 barrier, but the people still respond like members of a small church. They make decisions for the present and the future with no hope or anticipation of growing larger. Their de facto prophecies thus become self-fulfilling.

Barrier #9: The Stepping-Stone Pastor

In our recent study of evangelistic and high-assimilation churches, we made a startling discovery. Pastors in these effective or growing churches had a tenure *four times greater* than the general population of pastors.[14]

In my denomination, the Southern Baptist Convention, the average pastoral tenure is a woeful two years and three months. But the Southern Baptist churches that are growing evangelistically and retaining their growth have pastors with an average tenure of nine years and ten months![15]

Obviously a church cannot sustain consistent growth with new pastoral leadership every two to three years. Pastors are leaving their congregations after such a short stay for a variety of reasons. In some cases, the churches are force-terminating the pastor or pressuring him to leave. However, in some of the churches the pastor views his present place of ministry as a short-term stepping-stone to a larger church. He is unable and unwilling to make the long-term decisions for sustained growth in the church. And he may be unable and unwilling to make those decisions of incremental change because the ultimate change needed will take longer than he plans to stay.

Barrier #10: Staff Shortage

Many middle-sized churches are reluctant to add staff. Their excuses are legion. The most common, of course, is the concern about the financial cost of new personnel. But the shortage of ministry leadership is much more costly than expenditure to add staff.

Barrier #11: The Mission/Purpose Predicament

When my friend Rick Warren wrote *The Purpose Driven Church*,[16] the response to the book was amazing. Indeed the book is now one of the all-time best-sellers in its genre. What responsive chord did Rick strike when writing this book? On the one hand, the growth of Saddleback Valley Community Church is an amazing story. That could explain some of the interest in his book. But other pastors have written about their growing churches and have not received this level of response.

The issue that Rick seems to have addressed is the very basic issue of why the church exists. To use his words, he addresses the purpose of the church and insists that the church be "purpose driven."

I naively assumed that most active church members would know that the purposes of the church include worship, evangelism, discipleship, ministry, and fellowship. But I was surprised when our study revealed that less than one out of ten members could name all five purposes of the church. And less than one out of four named evangelism as one of the purposes of the church![17]

How can we expect churches to grow beyond certain barriers if its members cannot even articulate why the church exists? Why should they be motivated to evangelize when such a small minority understands evangelism to be a purpose of the church?

Although this issue came up eleventh in frequency in our interviews, I suspect it is a deeper problem than most of us realize. We will address the mission/purpose dilemma in some detail in the next chapter.

Barrier #12: The Ex-Neighborhood Church

Three of the next five barriers have been addressed by C. Peter Wagner in his book *The Healthy Church*. The ex-neighborhood church is also called "ethnikitis" by Wagner.[18] It is a church whose membership no longer reflects the community in which it is located.

Perhaps the most common manifestation is an Anglo church in a neighborhood that has transitioned from predominately Anglo to predominately African-American. Those members who have chosen to remain with the church find themselves either unable or unwilling to reach residents of the community who have a different racial or cultural background than they do. The church is headed for certain decline or death without major intervention.

Many middle-sized churches in America are confronted with this barrier. Sadly, most will die within several years. The common alternatives are to relocate, to relinquish leadership to the new community, or to die.

Barrier #13: Finite Facilities Syndrome

Wagner calls this barrier (or "disease," to use his terminology) sociological strangulation.[19] Simply stated, the church has run out of room to accommodate further growth. The shortage of space may be in parking, the sanctuary/worship center, the Sunday School area, or the preschool area.

Churches in this situation must realize that they have finite space and must choose one of several options to continue growing. We will look at those options in the next chapter.

Barrier #14: "Fundingitis"

Churches that move from being small to becoming middle-sized often discover funds that have never before been available. The pattern of the past was to use every dollar to pay bills of necessity and urgency. Now, with new growth, additional funds are in the budget. How should they be used?

A conflict over how to spend the additional money can become a significant barrier to growth. Many people have many different ideas about how to utilize the resources. If the conflict is too severe, the distraction can become so great that growth is halted.

Barrier #15: The Dissenting Minority

I consulted with a church several years ago that had successfully broken two barriers: the Power Group Syndrome and the not-like-us malady. The majority of the members were motivated and excited about the church moving forward in growth.

Over the course of several months, however, the former power group became vocal again in its opposition to the leadership. Rather than move forward, as they had done in the past, the new majority began to spend an inordinate amount of time responding to the dissenting minority. The church's growth stopped, and the strong momentum of past months all but disappeared.

Barrier #16: Ghost Town Disease

Another Wagner-coined term, Ghost Town Disease, refers to sick churches in communities that are dying.[20] The population is steadily declining with little or no hope of recovery. The churches quite naturally suffer the decline that is taking place in their communities. Growth in these churches is difficult, if not impossible, because the population base has dwindled to the point that few or no prospective new members are available.

The Bundle of Barriers

The middle-sized church may face more barriers than the small or large church. The reasons for this predicament are twofold. First, middle-sized churches represent a wide range of sizes. One middle-sized church may have 250 in attendance while another has 800. On the spectrum of church sizes, the middle-sized churches comprise a wide range.

It is thus understandable that the various churches of different sizes will encounter a breadth of barriers. The challenge is first to identify the barriers so that solutions can be posed.

Second, middle-sized churches may sometimes "act" like small churches, sometimes like large churches, or sometimes like neither. It is not inconceivable for a group of middle-sized churches to face *all* the barriers mentioned in this book.

After over five years of researching nearly 2,000 churches of various denominations, backgrounds, locations, and sizes, my research team at the Billy Graham School at Southern Seminary in Louisville has identified ten key issues for churches to grow evangelistically. All ten points will not apply to all churches, but many will.

In the next chapter we will look at these key issues and apply them to the middle-sized church. We will also ask a few key questions to help you determine if your church needs to make some changes to move beyond the next barrier. Join me in the next pages as we examine the "ten-point checkup for growth barriers."

CHAPTER FIVE

The Middle-Sized Church: A Ten-Point Checkup to Break Growth Barriers

Imagine this scenario: more than 1,000 churches of various sizes, backgrounds, and locations that are among the most evangelistic growth churches in our nation. Many of them were once plateaued or declining; now they are alive and vibrant, with new Christians in their midst. You have the opportunity to ask them the pragmatic question: "How?" How did they move past growth barriers to become the dynamic, growing churches they are today?

Such is the opportunity I have had over the past five years. My team at the Graham School and I have devoted much of our lives to studying churches that are growing significantly by conversions.[1] Through the generous gifts of endowed funds, we have been able to study hundreds of churches through surveys, interviews, and on-site visits.

For this chapter, I looked only at the churches with an average attendance between 200 and 700. I wanted to review the data that particularly applied to middle-sized churches. The results were fascinating.

I was able to find ten major ways that middle-sized churches have overcome growth barriers. I call these ten items a "ten-point checkup to growth barriers."

Checkup #1: The Preaching Phenomenon

Overcomes which barriers?

- Comfortitis
- Biblical blindness
- Small-church mentality
- The mission/purpose predicament
- Ministry misplacement

Perhaps one of the most overlooked and "underdiscussed" issues in church growth today is the relationship between preaching and church growth. In our research we found that preaching was the leading issue in the conversion growth of the church.

When we compared over 300 evangelistic churches to a similar number of nongrowing churches, we found several significant differences. One of the most significant differences was discovered when we asked the pastors: "How much time, on the average, do you spend in sermon preparation per sermon each week?" The pastors of the nongrowing churches averaged slightly over two hours of preparation time per sermon. The pastors in the high-conversion growth churches averaged *ten hours per sermon each week*!

This fivefold difference in sermon preparation time was among the biggest differences in the two groups of churches. Indeed, many pastors told us they had seen their church break growth barriers when they returned to the apostolic priority noted in Acts 6:4: "'But we will devote ourselves to prayer and to *the ministry of the word*'" (NASB, emphasis added).

The number of activities and responsibilities of the pastor can be unlimited in a middle-sized church. He can be found doing anything from janitorial work to denominational activities.

Several years ago I gave a survey to the twelve deacons of a church in St. Petersburg, Florida, where I served as pastor. I simply listed several categories of pastoral responsibilities and asked them to share with me a *minimum* amount of time that should be spent on each responsibility. If I had met the *minimum* expectations of just the twelve deacons, my workweek would be as follows:

Prayer	14 hours
Sermon preparation	18 hours
Outreach visitation	10 hours
Counseling	10 hours
Hospital/home visitation	15 hours
Administration	18 hours
Community involvement	5 hours
Denominational involvement	5 hours
Church meetings	5 hours
Worship services	4 hours
Other	10 hours
	114 hours/week[2]

Obviously no one can sustain a 114-hour workweek. And the numbers above represent the expectations of only twelve deacons. Imagine the length of pastors' workweeks if they met all the church members' expectations! But quite often pastors in middle-sized churches do find themselves trying to please everyone. And the two easiest responsibilities to neglect are prayer and sermon preparation. No one is watching the pastor during these times; yet our studies found that pastors who gave these areas priority were those who pastored the most evangelistic churches.

As pastors spend more time in God's Word, they are able to preach with more authority, knowledge, and conviction. The Holy Spirit uses the preached Word to move churches out of their comfort zones and to move them to a greater obedience to God's truths.

Faithful and well-prepared preaching helps church members to see that a certain small size is not necessarily God's ideal. Indeed they see that they are to be constantly reaching others whatever their size may be. They cannot maintain a small-church mentality when the fullness of God's Word is proclaimed.

Powerful preaching helps the church to understand its purpose more clearly. And as we shall see shortly, churches that know their purpose or mission are much more likely to overcome barriers than churches that are ignorant of their mission.

Preaching is one of the chief equipping approaches of the pastor. As he faithfully proclaims God's Word every week, the members of the church begin to understand that they are indeed to do the work of ministry. The barrier of ministry misplacement is thus often overcome through powerful preaching.

Of course, virtually every church has preaching in its worship services. The key differences in evangelistic churches are the *centrality* of preaching and the time the pastor gives to the preparation of his messages.

Checkup #2: A Praying People

Overcomes which barriers?

- Comfortitis
- Participatory democracy
- Power Group Syndrome
- Not-like-us malady
- The dissenting minority

Very few people have studied and written about prayer in the church more than Peter Wagner. In many ways I feel that his words should be the source of expertise for this section. My other coauthor, Elmer Towns, has also written extensively on prayer and fasting.

Perhaps I have made a small contribution to the literature of local church prayer through the data-filled studies conducted by the Billy Graham School at Southern Seminary. One inescapable conclusion we have noted in all of our studies is that prayer is vital in the growth of the church.

Bill Hohenstreet is pastor of the Post Falls Baptist Church in Post Falls, Idaho. The attendance is now breaking the 200 barrier. Listen to his words describing the importance of prayer at his church: "We keep a prayer list for salvation. The interesting thing is that a member cannot place a person's name on that list without first witnessing to that person."[3]

Pastor Hohenstreet excitedly told us of the results of this prayer emphasis: "The church now has 4,000 names on this list [remember, this church has two hundred in attendance], which means that at least that many soul-winning confrontations have taken place. After a person is converted, the name stays on the list as the church continues to pray for real spiritual growth."[4]

One major factor that affected the growth of the churches was that the praying people became changed people. The pastor of a middle-sized church in Florida said: "Our church was about as unified as the Hatfields and McCoys. The people disagreed and fought about almost everything. That is, until our prayer ministry began. Slowly at first, but then without any doubt, our members' attitudes began to change."

Indeed some of the greatest barriers to growth in a church are attitudinal. The five barriers shown on the previous page are among those barriers to growth.

What does prayer do in a church? When a church emphasizes and organizes an intercessory prayer ministry, the focus of those praying moves from self to God and others. A servant attitude develops that is more concerned about the kingdom than getting one's own way in the church. Instead of seeing how much control they can exert, intercessors often desire to see how much service they can render.

Prayer intercessors are more likely to see others through the eyes of God. They are less likely to reject others just because they are not like them, and they are less likely to resist change just because it is change. Repeatedly and without question, a praying church is a church that has already begun to overcome several significant barriers.

Checkup #3: Focusing Outward

Overcomes which barriers?

• Comfortitis

• The pastoral care pastor

• The mission/purpose predicament

• Fundingitis

One of the first steps I take when I consult with a church is to ask the leaders to identify all the outward foci of the church. How much of their budget is devoted to ministry beyond the membership of the church? What proportion of the activities explicitly seek to evangelize and reach out to those not in the church? How much of the pastor's and staff's time is spent in evangelism or equipping others to reach out?

A typical response is one of surprise and disappointment. As a Wesleyan pastor in Idaho recently told me: "It's no wonder my church has reached a barrier. We're not doing much to overcome it."

The next step I take in these consultations is to bring as much of the membership together as is feasible, divide them into groups, and ask them to brainstorm about ways their church can focus outward. An amazing phenomenon usually takes place.

The members stop talking about "my needs" and "what I like" and start developing a Great Commission mind-set. They begin to realize that reaching out is part of the mission and the purpose of the church. And they develop ideas about where their budget and funds can be used to have an outward focus in the community and beyond.

The pastor often catches the excitement as well. One well-loved pastor of a church in Oklahoma asked me to come into his office. He confided that his "security blanket" was meeting members' needs exclusively. He confessed that their affirmation was his primary motivator. But then he said in a broken voice: "Thom, this exercise has shown me that I have not been obedient to the Great Commission. I have to develop my own outward focus."

Many middle-sized churches have ceased to grow because their energies and resources have become more and more devoted to maintenance rather than growth. An honest evaluation and an outward focus can often bring dramatic change.

Checkup #4: The Mission/ Purpose Mindset

Overcomes which barriers?

- Biblical blindness
- The mission/purpose predicament

- Fundingitis
- Staff shortage

The late Donald McGavran is one of my heroes of the faith. The father of the Church Growth Movement had a passion for disciple-making, whether on the mission field abroad or in churches in America. McGavran insisted that biblically obedient churches seek to grow by conversion growth and the new Christians become fruit-bearing disciples in the local church.

According to our research, very few churches in America would meet the criteria that McGavran said was critically important to church growth. Few would have significant conversion growth and fewer would see that new growth retained over the course of several years.

Our studies also revealed that the few churches that are experiencing and retaining conversion growth have a common denominator: the people of the churches understand the biblical purposes or mission of the church.

For review, remember how our research distinguished between *mission* and *vision*. *Mission* was defined as "the primary purpose in which all Christian churches should be involved; these purposes typically include worship, evangelism, discipleship, ministry, and fellowship."[5] "Vision" was "God's *specific* plan for a *specific* church at a *specific* time."[6]

Our research team was honestly expecting the "vision" issue to be a major distinguishing factor between evangelistic and non-evangelistic churches. Much to our surprise, "vision" was not a distinguishing factor, but "mission" was. Those churches that were reaching and keeping new Christians clearly understood their biblical purpose.

For example, a majority of the members in evangelistic churches could name all five purposes of the church. In the non-evangelistic churches, only *10 percent* of the members named evangelism as a purpose of the church! Little wonder that the latter churches were reaching few or none for Christ.

A church that understands its mission understands the biblical basis for the church. The members are not blind to the biblical mandates they must follow. These churches allocate resources of people, time, and money in order to be biblically balanced churches. They know why the church exists and what they need to do to be faithful to God's commands.

Our research team was indeed surprised to discover the ignorance that exists in many churches over the basic mission of the church. And the churches that had addressed this ignorance were highly intentional about educating their members on the five purposes.

The word we heard often was *redundancy*. Through preaching, teaching, testimonies, newsletter articles, slogans, mottoes, and so on, the churches were constantly being informed as to the reason for their existence and to that which must be done to be biblically obedient.

Checkup #5: The Eyes of the Outsider

Overcomes which barriers?

- Comfortitis
- Not-like-us malady
- Staff shortage
- Finite Facilities Syndrome
- Fundingitis

In a church I served as pastor several years ago, we had an interesting exercise. Twice a year we would give a nonmember a form that included an extensive listing of all of our church facilities, building by building, room by room. The person was asked to note her observations as she looked at our facilities for the first time. We were amazed at how much we overlooked just because we saw our building and grounds every day. We would then take the following six months to make changes where possible.

Middle-sized churches that are overcoming growth barriers are devising innovative ways to get their people to look at their churches through the eyes of an outsider. A church in Michigan asks its members to visit another church at least once a year and note their experiences. How did you find the parking? Were entryways clearly marked? Did you feel welcomed? Why or why not? Did you feel awkward and out of place? Would you like to return?

By asking these questions of themselves, members are able to see their own churches in a different light. They begin to view other people in a way that desires to include them and make them feel welcome. They are able to make wise decisions about future staff, new or remodeled facilities, additional services, and other matters from the perspective of both the members and those on the "outside." Funding decisions are not based solely on what the members want for themselves but also on how to reach others.

We found that churches that intentionally and repetitively sought to have the eyes of the outsider were among the middle-sized churches that most often overcame barriers. A pastor in California was representative of leaders who had led their churches to have the eyes of the outsider: "We failed to move beyond 300 in attendance consistently until we sent four different people each week to different churches for twenty-six consecutive weeks. After six months, over one hundred people had been a visitor in another church. Boy, did that make a difference in our congregation!"

Checkup #6: The Acts 6 Solution

Overcomes which barriers?

- Ministry misplacement
- The pastoral care pastor
- Staff shortage

One of the greatest gifts I have ever received was given to me when I served as pastor of a church in Birmingham, Alabama. The average attendance of the church was 500, a large middle-sized church. But the church was positioned to become a large church with a few right decisions. One of those decisions was the gift I just mentioned.

Some of the leaders in the church came to me and told me they wanted to protect my study and prayer time. From then on my mornings were set aside for prayer and sermon preparation. The laity would take more responsibility for ministry, while I devoted more time to prayer and the ministry of the Word.

I believe that this decision was the most important in moving our church beyond a middle-sized barrier ultimately to become a large church. This Acts 6 Solution is exactly what happened in this church and also in the early church, when the needs of some of the widows were being overlooked.

The apostolic twelve made a decision to turn over the ministry of waiting on the widows to seven laymen. The apostles then focused their attention on prayer and the ministry of the Word (Acts 6:14). The results for the Jerusalem church are noted in Acts 6:7. They were threefold. First, the Word of God continued to spread. Second, more disciples were added to the church. And third, some of the hardest to reach, the Jewish priests, also became followers of Christ.

No middle-sized church will move beyond barriers until it consistently practices the Acts 6 solution. Remember, checkup #1 was "the preaching phenomenon." Pastors of growing churches devoted five times as many hours in sermon preparation than the pastors of nongrowing churches. But, if the pastor spends that much more time in the ministry of the Word, the ministry of the church must not suffer. The laity must answer their God-given call to do the work of ministry.

After my church in Birmingham urged me to spend adequate time in the ministry of the Word, we took the next step in better equipping the laity to do the work of ministry. We began an intensive emphasis and training in spiritual gifts discovery and implementation. People in the church became more and more involved in ministry, according to their giftedness and their passions.

The Acts 6 solution is absolutely critical for a middle-sized church to break growth barriers. We discovered this solution in both my own ministry and in the ministry of the laity of the church. Indeed, I am convinced that the church would have never become a large church without the concerted effort of our people. And I am likewise convinced from the data we gathered in our research that this step is critical for successful middle-sized churches.

Checkup #7: The High-Expectation Church

Overcomes which barriers?

- Comfortitis
- Biblical blindness
- The Mission/Purpose Predicament
- Ministry misplacement

In our studies of over 1,000 effective evangelistic churches, a consistent theme ran through almost all of our survey responses. The churches that were experiencing significant evangelistic growth and effective assimilation had high expectations of their members. The churches communicated clearly that membership was equivalent to ministry rather than being a name on a roll. And they communicated that people in the body of Christ should be faithful in their ministries, gifts, and activities in the church.

In a typical church, only about 40 percent of the members could be called true ministers. And if you include tithing, involvement in ministry, and regular attendance in worship and Sunday School as criteria for membership, only one out of seven church members would be on the rolls today.

Most churches in America today have done a poor job of placing biblical expectations upon their members. For many people, joining a church is little more than completing a card or walking down an aisle. This understanding of membership in the body of Christ certainly has no New Testament foundation!

How then does a church transition to become a high-expectation church? Most churches that have successfully made this transition have begun the process with a new members' class. Many of the churches require prospective members to complete the class prior to membership. Other churches expect or strongly encourage persons to complete the class.

Expectations of church membership can be clearly communicated in the new members' class. The prospective members can understand what it means to be a part of God's church. And they can know well that the church does not take their membership lightly.

In our study of new members' classes in effective evangelistic churches, we found numerous topics covered. Below are several examples. The percentages in parentheses represent the number of churches that included the item in their new members' classes.

- Doctrine of the church (67%)
- Polity of the church (66%)
- History of the church (57%)
- Requirements for membership (39%)
- Expectations of members (55%)
- Policies for discipline (63%)
- Witness training (19%)
- Training in spiritual disciplines (35%)
- Plan of salvation (49%)
- Examination of church covenant (63%)
- Teaching of spiritual gifts/spiritual gifts inventory (30%)
- Explanation of the church's mission and/or vision (33%)
- Facts about the denomination (52%)
- Ministry opportunities (37%)
- Tithing and financial support (76%)

The high-expectation church utilizes the new members' class to communicate clearly the biblical model of involvement in the local church. The barrier of comfortitis is overcome as the prospective members see clearly that idleness in the church is not an option. The barriers of biblical blindness and the mission/purpose predicament are overcome as clear biblical teachings are communicated through the class or other venues. And the ministry misplacement barrier is overcome when new members are routed to places of ministry according to their spiritual gifts and sense of God's calling to ministry.

Though our research was directed toward churches of all sizes, we found that the high expectation factor was particularly pertinent for the middle-sized church.[7] As a church grows from small to middle-sized, commitment of the members becomes increasingly important. If the church is to break different barriers and perhaps soon become a large church, this checkup is imperative.

Checkup #8: The Dinosaur Factor

Overcomes which barriers?

- Not-like-us malady
- Ministry misplacement
- The pastoral care pastor
- Biblical blindness
- The mission/purpose predicament

In the middle and late 1980s I was convinced that the Sunday School was a methodology of antiquity, a dinosaur headed for extinction. The program, I surmised, had served its purpose well, but now it was time to move to new and innovative approaches.

I then began doing research on growing churches across our nation, particularly growing evangelistic churches.[8] Much to my surprise, I discovered that well over 90 percent of these churches had strong and vibrant Sunday Schools. Now I can say without hesitation that a strong Sunday School is a critical need for the middle-sized church to overcome growth barriers.

Let us review for a moment a typical situation of a small church growing to middle-size, only to plateau in attendance for years. Most likely, a pastor and perhaps a few committed laypersons lead the growth in this small church. This small group of people is committed to outreach, evangelism, and ministry. Because of their work, a church may grow to middle-sized levels, only to see that growth stymied.

The problem is usually related to too much ministry for too few people. The resources of the middle-sized church become stretched to their limits. But our research has shown that the Sunday School is a barrier breaker in numerous respects. Let us look at some of the contributions a healthy Sunday School makes toward the growth of the church.

Biblical Education for All Ages

A few years ago a study of the Presbyterian Church (U.S.A.) concluded that the abandonment of biblical authority and the failure to teach those truths through Sunday School accounted for most of the decline in the mainline denomination. The essence of this fascinating research was that biblical education that reaches all age groups is a necessity.

The authors of this study lamented the demise of Sunday School in their denomination. "Today Presbyterians should not bemoan the lack of faith and church commitment . . . since they have no one to blame but themselves. No outside power forcibly pulled their children away from the faith. No conquering army or hostile missionaries destroyed the tradition. The Presbyterians made the decisions themselves, on one specific [doctrinal] issue after another, over the decades."[9]

Sunday School removes the barrier of biblical blindness. A healthy Sunday School will teach all ages the truths of Scripture and provide the church with a strong and certain foundation.

Ministry Opportunities

My research team at Southern Seminary has reviewed the data and interviews of nearly 2,000 churches across our nation. One inescapable conclusion about the healthy and growing churches is that these churches have a myriad of opportunities for the people to do ministry within the Sunday School.

Some of the Sunday School participants are care group leaders with direct ministry responsibilities for four or five people. Others are involved in outreach and evangelism through the Sunday School. Still others use their administrative gifts for organizational needs in the Sunday School.

A healthy Sunday School will overcome the barrier of ministry misplacement. This organization affords more people more opportunities for ministry than any other avenue in the churches we studied. The Sunday School, similarly, helps the church to overcome the mission/purpose predicament barrier because most of the church's purposes can be carried out here.

The Sunday School can be a tremendous blessing for the pastor who finds himself stretched to the limit with ministry demands. The church I pastored in St. Petersburg, Florida, had an outstanding Sunday School organization. When I arrived at a hospital or a home to meet a ministry need, I typically discovered that I had been preceded by Sunday School class members.

Eventually I learned that my indispensability was a myth. Ministry could take place without me. I was freed from the pastoral care-pastor barrier, and growth ensued.

A Place for (Most) Everyone

No church can meet the needs of all people. But the Sunday School organization, through a variety of classes, *can* offer a place where many people feel welcome. The barrier I called the not-like-us malady is often overcome through Sunday School.

Quality Is the Key

I have been surprised by the renewed interest in Sunday School in the past few years. Growing churches are rediscovering its effectiveness and comprehensiveness for ministry in the church. But a word of caution is in order. The mere existence of a Sunday School in a church does not mean the organization is effective. Quality is the key.

In a recent speaking engagement in the Washington, D.C. area, I spoke with the pastor of a fast-growing church where Sunday School had been rediscovered. Three years earlier, the leadership of the church decided to make Sunday School a top priority.

One of the first steps was to seek a high level of commitment from the teachers and other workers. Some balked, but those who remained became dedicated ministers in the Sunday School.

On Wednesday nights all of the teachers come together to preview the lesson. Outreach leaders make consistent visits and calls each week. Care group leaders make certain that those in their groups receive and participate in ministry. And administrative leaders keep the organization running smoothly.

Just a few years ago, this church was middle-sized with a significant "back door" or loss of members. Today worship attendance is 1,100 and Sunday School attendance is 1,000. Those who join the church rarely leave. Instead they get integrally "connected" to others through this "antiquated" organization called the Sunday School. The dinosaur lives and is functioning well![10]

Checkup #9: Eating the Elephant

Overcomes which barriers?

- Comfortitis
- Participatory democracy
- Power Group Syndrome

- The stepping-stone pastor
- The dissenting minority

Change is difficult. It seems to be especially difficult for members of middle-sized churches. We have already addressed the comfort level that is often inherent in these churches. The resources are such that programs and ministries can continue without severe financial strain. Unlike many small churches, the middle-sized church is able to make decisions of resource allocation beyond basic survival needs.

But the level of comfort is also related to interpersonal relationships. The members may not know one another well, but they still feel like a family. Said one layperson in our studies of middle-sized churches: "Our church is just the right size. Not so small that we can't do some things. And not so large that everyone seems like a stranger."[11]

This comfort level is sometimes evident in the members' desires to retain control or maintain the status quo, as earlier discussed in the sections on the barriers of comfortitis, participatory democracy, and the Power Group Syndrome. Or, if some members sense that the church is moving in a direction beyond their control or desire, they may present the barrier of the dissenting minority.

Hardly a day goes by that a pastor does not ask me how to approach these issues and obstacles: "I just can't get my members to follow my leadership," some say. Others lament, "There are just too many obstacles to growth."

In our research on middle-sized churches, we found a fascinating statistic on pastoral tenure. *Pastoral tenure in evangelistic and high-assimilation churches was four times higher than the tenure in nonevangelistic and nongrowing churches.* Pastors whose churches had successfully overcome the barriers related to control and fear of change demonstrated two clear characteristics: tenacity and a long-term outlook.

All the pastors we interviewed told stories of control groups or opposition to change. Their response was neither one of bulldozing nor retreat. Instead, they chose to make changes incrementally, taking the churches at the pace their members could best accept. Their leadership style was like eating an elephant; they took only one "bite" at a time.[12]

A clear example of the tenure issue and the long-term outlook of pastors was evident in our study of pastors in my denomination, the Southern Baptist Convention. Pastors of the evangelistic and growing Southern Baptist churches had an average tenure of nine years and ten months. But the overall average tenure of Southern Baptist pastors is less than three years.

The pastors who were able to overcome many of the growth barriers entered a new pastorate with a long-term view. Short-term setbacks were not viewed as tragic. Opposition was perceived to be temporary. These pastors could see their churches' futures well beyond the moment of the immediate crisis.

Obviously, pastors with the long-term perspective cannot see themselves in a "stepping-stone" situation. A pastor of a Wesleyan church in Idaho said it well: "I don't worry about moving to a larger church. God called me to this church to lead it to growth. I am free to think about this church's future ten years from now because I'm not worried about moving to a so-called better situation."[13]

Checkup #10: The Principle of Priority

Overcomes which barriers?

- Biblical blindness
- The mission/purpose predicament
- The dissenting minority
- The pastoral care pastor

In December 1997, Billy Graham commented on his life's passion: "Even a casual inspection of the New Testament will reveal that evangelism was the priority of the early church. Christians are called by God to do many things, but a church that has lost sight of the priority of evangelism has lost sight of its primary calling under God."[14]

The famed evangelist would lament that this priority is not evident in many churches today: "Sad to say, evangelism in many churches today (and for many individual Christians) seems almost an afterthought to the normal workings of the congregation or denomination."[15]

During the 1970s and 1980s, a debate ensued in scholarly circles about the priority of evangelism. Should evangelism be the forefront ministry? Does the Bible hold to a priority of evangelism? While the intellectual debate was taking place, many churches moved evangelism to a secondary issue. And those are the very churches that plateaued, declined, or found themselves facing insurmountable barriers.

Meanwhile, relatively few churches intentionally moved evangelism to a place of priority in their ministries and programs. Often these were the churches that were growing and breaking barriers.

In our survey of laypersons in growing churches, we asked them to name the purposes of the church. Over 90 percent named evangelism as one of the purposes. The members understood clearly the biblical mandate to make evangelism a priority.

Our research leaves us little doubt that an evangelistic priority in a church is one of the keys to breaking growth barriers. Not only do these churches have a sense of biblical obedience, they also possess a sense of excitement as new Christians come into the fellowship. These new Christians put the focus on evangelism rather than on negative people and ineffective ministries. Evangelism creates a momentum that builds and grows.

The pastor in an evangelistic-priority church will soon discover that he cannot lead in evangelism and do all the pastoral ministries that are often expected or demanded. If the priority of evangelism is to continue, he must not succumb to the pastoral-care barrier. The laity must do the work of ministry, while the pastor leads the church to reach people for Christ and to break new growth barriers.

Other Barriers to Break

Some of the barriers a middle-sized church faces are not unique for its size. The need for space, for example, is a common barrier at every size. The Finite Facilities Syndrome can be addressed through the building of new facilities, by offering multiple services, or by discovering innovative ways to utilize space.

Similarly, the barriers called the ex-neighborhood church and Ghost Town Disease are demographic barriers that are not unique to the middle-sized church. Possible approaches to these barriers have been discussed elsewhere in this book.

The Middle-Sized Church: Many Growth Barriers, Many Solutions

The small church has its own barriers because of its unique situation as a single-cell church. But the middle-sized church is a more complex organism with many possibilities that could explain why the growth has ceased. In the chapters you have just read, I have attempted to explain many of those barriers and how most of them can be overcome.

If you are a leader in a middle-sized church, I would encourage you to review the previous chapter and to do a church diagnosis. Gather eight to twelve key leaders in your church and review the barriers. Are some of these possible barriers in your church? Are some obviously present? Are others potential barriers? Which are the greatest barriers at this point?

Next, review the ten checkups in this chapter. Develop possible strategies to overcome the most significant barriers. Discuss the ease or difficulty that may be present as you attempt new strategies.

Develop priorities and timetables. And, above all, pray that God's Spirit may bring a true revival in the midst of this process.

A few churches grow dramatically and rapidly. These churches are typically featured in books and conferences. But our research shows that most churches that break barriers do so over a lengthy period. Be patient. Wait on God. And see what miracles he will bring!

PART 3

OVERCOMING LARGE CHURCH

BARRIERS OF 1,000 PEOPLE

BY

ELMER L. TOWNS

Elmer Towns wrote one of the first American church growth books in 1969. The editor of *Christian Life Magazine* described the book as "a thunder clap" that hit the evangelical world. The secular media had focused on struggling inner-city churches and home Bible studies. Towns brought optimistic news to Bible believers that God was growing churches, that the largest churches in America were committed to conservative beliefs, and that multitudes were getting saved through these large churches.

There were only 97 large churches—those with 1,000 or more in attendance in 1969 when Towns published his book. Today there are over 6,000 in America. One out of every 100 churches in America is a superchurch of mega proportions. In this section, Towns tells why the number of large churches has increased, why some churches have difficulties breaking into this elite level, and what a church has to do to break 1,000 and keep growing.

Elmer Towns holds a B.A. from Northwestern College; M.A., Southern Methodist University; Th.M., Dallas Theological Seminary; M.R.E, Garrett Theological Seminary; and D.Min., Fuller Theological Seminary. At age 65, he is returning to school to work on another doctorate in church growth because he wants to keep learning, and everything he learns, he will keep teaching, and everything he teaches, he will write. He lives with his wife Ruth in Lynchburg, Virginia, where he is dean of the School of Religion, Liberty University. They have three children and eight grandchildren.

CHAPTER SIX

The Emergence of Megachurches

In 1967, I was teaching a class at Trinity Evangelical Divinity School, Greater Chicago, Illinois, when I asked, "What is the largest church in the United States?" To answer my question, I suggested to the class that it was the First Baptist Church, Dallas, Texas, pastored by W. A. Criswell. I told the class that when I attended the church, it had an attendance of approximately 4,000. I remember Dr. Criswell saying it was probably the largest church in the world.

A student put his hand up to suggest that First Baptist Church, Hammond, Indiana, pastored by Dr. Jack Hyles was larger. I disagreed with the student, because the Hammond church had 2,500 in attendance, which was smaller than the Dallas church.

"But Dr. Jack Hyles claims that his is the largest church in the world," the student explained.

"You can't always believe the attendance figures cited by pastors," I countered.

Everyone laughed.

At this point, a student in the back put his hand up to say that a church in Akron, Ohio, was the largest in the world. The student explained that the pastor claimed his church was the largest, and the student thought attendance was approximately 6,000.

The discussion took another direction, and our conversation about the largest church was dropped. I didn't think about the topic again until the next Sunday afternoon when I was reading the list of the ten best-selling books of the week in the Chicago *Tribune*. The thought crossed my mind, "What are the ten largest churches in America?" I determined to find the ten largest churches and to list them in order.

At the time I was Sunday School editor of *Christian Life Magazine*, Wheaton, Illinois. The magazine was the largest selling in the Christian world in 1967. I proposed a major article on the ten largest Sunday Schools in America and set out to discover them. Since Sunday School attendance was maintained at most churches, but not worship attendance, I focused my research on the Sunday School. I wrote all denominations and contacted the major Sunday School conventions, which would have been located in most of the major cities of America. Then we printed ads in the pages of *Christian Life Magazine*, asking readers to help us discover and identify the ten largest Sunday Schools in America.

True to the student's words, the largest Sunday School in America was Akron Baptist Temple, Akron, Ohio, with an average weekly attendance of 5,762 pupils. No one had ever listed the largest churches in order, and according to Robert Walker, editor of *Christian Life Magazine*, "The news hit the evangelical world like a thunder clap."[1]

The average Christian thought churches were dying and that vibrant soul-winning churches were declining, especially churches deeply committed to conservative doctrines. Because most media were giving coverage to denominational churches, many of them in a dying inner-city era, no one thought the churches of America outside metropolitan areas were vibrant and growing. In the mid-1960s many people thought that the home Bible studies would be the wave of the future. The book, *The Ten Largest Sunday Schools*,[2] changed the thinking of most Americans about the megachurch and ushered in an era of public concentration on large churches.

America's Ten Largest Sunday Schools, 1969, and Their Attendance[3]

1.	Akron Baptist Temple, Akron, Ohio,	5,762
2.	Highland Park Baptist Church, Chattanooga, Tennessee	4,821
3.	First Baptist Church, Dallas, Texas	4,731
4.	First Baptist Church, Hammond, Indiana	3,978
5.	Canton Baptist Temple, Canton, Ohio	3,581
6.	Landmark Baptist Church, Cincinnati, Ohio	3,540
7.	Temple Baptist Church, Detroit, Michigan	3,400
8.	First Baptist Church, Van Nuys, California	2,847
9.	Thomas Road Baptist Church, Lynchburg, Virginia	2,640
10.	Calvary Temple, Denver, Colorado	2,453

The list of the ten largest Sunday Schools came out of a larger list, that is, the list of the 100 largest Sunday Schools. In 1967, only 97 Sunday Schools in America averaged 1,000 or more in weekly attendance.[4] However, thirty years later (1997) over 6,000 churches or Sunday Schools in America have a weekly attendance of 1,000 or more. The list of churches in the United States with an average attendance of 1,000 or more is compiled by an informal survey of those who are knowledgeable of the large-church movement. This list includes all churches: independent, denominational, ethnic minority, and foreign language churches.

Obviously, an explosion of megachurches has occurred in the United States. Many reasons can be cited for the burgeoning number of these large churches. Some of the reasons have been categorized and are suggested in the following pages.

Why the Growth of Megachurches?

1. *The Internet and Interstate.*[5] These are symbolic words. The term *Interstate* stands for travel. The highway system of cities and states has given people access to churches. The *Internet* stands for communication. As people learn about the benefits of the megachurches, they seek them out and attend their services. While there are several other external reasons for their dramatic appearance on our stage in the last thirty years, most of these reasons are implications of the Interstate and Internet.

The word *Internet* stands for communication. Church planters have learned about megachurches, and they intentionally seek to plant them. Next, existing pastors have learned about megachurches, and they apply principles from them to build their congregations into megachurches. Laypeople have also learned about them, and they have become churches of choice for some church attenders in America. Media in general, both Christian and secular, have given attention to these churches through articles, books, telecasts, and general references. They have publicized their numbers, growth, and innovative ideas. Finally, these churches have pioneered the cutting-edge ministries, using radio, television, and other media services to evangelize and minister to the public. Obviously, when their worship services are viewed through the media, their strengths and contributions are magnified. Then people learn about them and seek them out, making them even larger.

Books and seminars by church leaders and pastors of these large churches have given attention to the megachurch. The Thomas Road Baptist Church of Lynchburg, Virginia, has hosted a seminar called "Super Conference" whereby people are invited to come and learn principles of superaggressive evangelism, that is, using every available means to reach every available person at every available time.[6] The underlying appeal is that you can build a church as large as Thomas Road Baptist Church by following the principles used there. Also, books like *The Purpose Driven Church*[7] by Rick Warren, pastor of Saddleback Valley Community Church, Mission Viejo, California, present principles by which megachurches are planted and thrive. Rick Warren planted this church in 1980, and eighteen years later it has surpassed 10,000 in weekly attendance.

Obviously the word *Interstate* means more than expressways; it stands for the vast system of American transportation. Because of interstates, Americans travel farther, more frequently, and without barriers, that is, they have little concern or anxiety going on long trips for shopping, relaxation, vacations, or even work. Therefore, the Interstate system has made Americans travel friendly. Thus, it is possible for a citizen to travel up to a hundred miles to commute back and forth to work by car or train. I recently ran across a man who commuted to his employment from Long Island, New York, to the downtown loop of Chicago. When I asked him why, he answered that he had to make money in Chicago, but Long Island was his boyhood home and that was where he wanted to live, and cost was no factor. Because of *interstates*, today the average American will commute as far to church as he commutes to work.

Before World War II, many Americans walked three or four blocks to their neighborhood church because they were city dwellers. Obviously, those in the country would commute, but many of them not more than ten miles to their rural church. As a rule of thumb, Americans probably commuted as far to church as they did to work, to buy groceries, or to do weekly shopping. However, after World War II, when their mental restrictions to travel were broken, they began to travel across town to church, sometimes traveling twenty or thirty miles.

For years a couple traveled from Washington, D.C., to Lynchburg, Virginia, to attend my church. They left home at 5 A.M. every Sunday morning. This retired couple was in their sixties when I asked them why they came so far for worship service. The wife responded, "When you get to be my age, and nothing else in life is as important as going to church, distance is not an issue." The husband told me it was 164 miles from his driveway to our church parking lot, and they made the trip every weekend during good weather. When he died, she moved to Lynchburg to enter a nursing home so she could be brought to my church by bus each week.

2. *Technology of Boomers.* As superchurches in America have grown, so has the baby boomer generation, that is, those born between 1946 and 1966. As this generation came to American churches, they brought with them a commitment to technology, its use, its development, and its excellence. As church crowds got larger, church auditoriums got larger. This mandated an increase in amplification systems, hence better use of microphones (lapel mikes, directional mikes, etc.). Today some sound systems cost a quarter of a million dollars. Next came the need to communicate with a larger clientele. Therefore, the boomer leaders began using computer technology for mailing lists, desktop publishing, and communication with their members. On the heels of this came the use of the fax, cell phones by pastors, and E-mail. Earlier, the megachurches had begun using radio, television, and other forms of media. Many megachurches have television studios that rival local broadcast studio quality, not to mention radio stations and transmission devices. Many of these churches have their own radio and television stations. Furthermore, they now have Web pages and communicate through cable television.[8]

3. *Boomer Team Leadership.* As the boomers came on the scene, they brought a new concept of leadership. This new concept grew out of the way they were reared and the world into which they entered. Whereas the builder generation (those born before 1945) used traditional leadership principles, that is, the managing leader or

the downward cycle of leadership, the boomers came along with team leadership and upward styles of management philosophy.

Perhaps it all began when the boomers were watching the Mouseketeers as children. Rather than being raised on the isolated singers their parents had been raised on, such as Bing Crosby, Vaughn Monroe, Patti Page, Doris Day, and Dinah Shore, boomers began singing in groups like the Mouseketeers. This musical group was followed by the Monkeys, the Beatles, the Platters, the Supremes, and the Mamas and the Papas. One person estimated that the boomers and/or busters listened to more than 100,000 singing groups. Not necessarily a cause and effect, but surely a correlation—boomers learned to lead by teams rather than in isolated roles of leadership. Also, they watched the *Magnificent Seven* at the movies and learned about the "A-Team," "Star Trek," "Charlie's Angels," and "Mission Impossible." They learned that technological jobs got done by teamwork wherein each person contributed to the success of the team by offering his particular expertise or authority. So boomers brought to local church administration an understanding of spiritual gifts, perhaps better than any other generation; they realized that individuals on the pastoral staff each contributed to the health and growth of a church. Thus, pastoral team leadership was only natural for them.

The growth of many megachurches would not have been possible prior to World War II because of a limited view of isolated leadership. One senior pastor can build church attendance only so large; very few individuals can build a church to 1,000 and continue ministering to all the members. But boomers brought delegation and shared leadership into megachurches. They not only wanted to delegate some of their ministry to others on their staff, they did it. One reason for the growth of such a large number of large churches is the change in attitudes toward pastoral leadership. No one pastor can minister to all the needs of many people in the church, but through a team effort, many individuals can be helped, producing growth in local churches that make possible breaking the 1,000 barrier.

4. *The Science of Church Growth.*[9] Prior to World War II, people thought of growth in churches primarily in terms of numbers, that is, growing from 100 to 200 in attendance or membership. However, under the influence of Donald McGavran, the modern father of the Church Growth Movement, a new emphasis on discovering, clarifying, and applying the principles of church growth arose. These principles are the laws to grow a church. When leaders follow these laws/principles, their churches grow. Out of the Church Growth Movement came a multitude of books explaining the principles of how to grow a church, and, at the same time, books on barriers and diseases of church growth. People wanting to grow a church read these books and articles and attended conferences/conventions. Then they went home and began to grow churches by these principles.

Prior to World War II, when a pastor built a church that surpassed 100 or 1,000, he learned by trial and error and, because he was an outstanding individual, overcame many barriers along the way. However, most of these men did not write out their methodology, nor was it tested scientifically and written in a systematic form. These pastors of large churches usually published in the realm of sermons, commentaries, or other types of articles and books. As a result, they took their knowledge and principles of how to grow a church to the grave with them. Also, prior to World War II, courses on pastoral theology and/or ministry did not emphasize church growth, nor was the average candidate going through college or seminary exposed to church growth principles. Hence, these pastors were not challenged to build large churches, nor did they know how. But as the Church Growth Movement grew and became more influential, the number of megachurches also grew and became more influential.

5. *Shopping Center Mentality.* Before World War II, people shopped at a general store on the corner, or they took a bus downtown to do their shopping. The stores were all individual stores, usually near the businesses, government offices, legal courts, and banks. But after World War II, the automobile changed the way

we lived. Shopping centers sprouted up near new subdivisions. A shopping center was not necessarily the downtown store moved to suburbia. The term *synergism* described the energy of a shopping center, that is, multiple forces producing explosive energy that led to exponential growth. When three or four large "anchor" stores moved into a shopping center, which was surrounded by a multitude of smaller specialty stores, the results attracted a vastly larger number of shoppers, leading to explosive sales and profits for all the stores.

Building on the paradigm of synergism,[10] the megachurch is more than just a church of 1,000 or more in attendance. A megachurch has a synergism of multiple ministries all interrelating (*interphasing* is the new term) to produce explosive attendance growth. These multiple ministries are counseling centers, bus ministries, Christian schools K-12, Christian colleges, seminaries, day care centers, nursing homes, hospitals, cemeteries, singles' ministries, ministries to special needs groups (divorce, AIDS, sexual addiction, alcohol addiction, etc.), recreational ministries (age-graded teams, gyms, football fields, soccer fields, baseball diamonds, weight rooms, handball courts, bowling lanes, etc.), and activities for almost every age group, every type of hobby, leisure-time activity, etc.

Synergism is a powerful force that has allowed for the appearance of megachurches, some of which were built originally on evangelism, but whose large attendances are maintained by the interactive allegiance of members to one another through attendance at various activities.

6. *Multicampus Ministry.*[11] With the growth of transportation, communication, and new expressions of leadership, it was only natural that churches could operate in several locations at one time. Prior to World War II, only a few pastors would hurry from campus to campus so they could preach in each of the worship services. Suspicion and/or lack of ability to delegate kept churches from offering their ministry in more than one location.

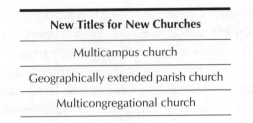

New Titles for New Churches
Multicampus church
Geographically extended parish church
Multicongregational church

One description for a large church is "multiministries, multi-ministers, and multiplaces of ministry." This definition implies the eventual emergence of multicampus churches. In an earlier book, Randy Pope is described going to Atlanta, Georgia, to plant one local church that would meet in 100 locations. He wanted to situate his 100 locations along the perimeter interstate around the city; hence he named the church Perimeter Presbyterian Church. With time, he wanted to appeal to a broader range of people so he dropped the title *Presbyterian.* Today it is called Perimeter Church. This type of church has the following characteristics: (1) geographically extended, (2) reflects a new strategy in leadership, (3) has the characteristics of a boomer church, (4) uses innovative scheduling, and (5) reflects the emergence of a new kind of denominationalism.

The Past

Many people have studied the large church. I appreciate the work of John Vaughan, *The Large Church: A Twentieth Century Expression of the First Century Church.* This is a valuable study of large churches because of its historical context. Vaughan shows that many large churches existed in the first century. He does not look to Christian church buildings to prove his point but uses a unique research approach to demonstrate that Christians worshiped in Jewish synagogues that were opened to them because Christians were considered by many to be a sect of the Hebrews. As such, Vaughan surveyed several synagogues that accommodated 10,000 in attendance. He then goes on to survey history and shows that large churches have existed in every century. But there has never been a period of time when so many large churches appeared as in the past thirty years.

Several names have been coined for the large church. Technically, this section deals with those having over 1,000 in attendance, even though many count by membership (which implies a lower attendance). Vaughan wants to call a megachurch one that has 2,000 or more in attendance, but in popular terminology that designation may not have caught on. Many still refer to 1,000 as a megachurch. Also, Carl George used the title *metachurch* to describe congregations of 10,000 that are cell-driven.[12] Because of confusion in the minds of many and the fact that the term didn't catch on with the public, the term *metachurch* is not a reference point in this book. However, for the sake of reference, the term will be used interchangeably (see below).

	Names for the Large Church
1	Megachurch (numbers)
2	Superchurch (type of evangelism)
3	Large church (size)
4	Geographically extended parish church (geography)
5	Extended campus church (location)
6	Multicongregational church (sociological)
7	Age-graded and gender-graded Sunday School (education)
8	Metachurch (strategy of cells for growth)

To Take Away

A goal of 1,000 is a wonderful aim, if your heart is pure and you have your priorities in order. A pastor must never attempt to break 1,000 just for personal satisfaction or because it is a numerical goal. You grow a church past 1,000 because you want to reach more people for Jesus Christ. You cast a vision of breaking 1,000 because Jesus Christ said, "Go ye therefore and make disciples of all nations" (Matt. 28:19 KJV), and "Preach the gospel to every creature" (Mark 16:15 KJV). You sacrifice to break 1,000 because you want to obey Jesus and bring glory to the Father.

Nothing is magical about 1,000; it doesn't make the church better, more godly, or even more efficient. The goal of 1,000 is just one step in a lifelong journey of serving God and ministering for him. Actually, you don't want to stop at 1,000, as just mentioned; 1,000 is only a step on your journey.

CHAPTER SEVEN

Why the 1,000
Barrier Is Difficult

Thirty years ago I was gathering statistics to find the 100 largest churches in America. It seemed that every time I found a church with 1,000 or more in attendance, I also found many churches with almost 1,000 in attendance, which just couldn't get beyond the 1,000 barrier. There seemed to be 100 churches right under 1,000 for each church that broke the 1,000 barrier.[1] I kept asking myself, "Why is the 1,000 barrier so hard to break?"

Obviously, the exact 1,000 statistical number is not a magical barrier, but there are inhibiting barriers for this size that make it difficult to break. Some churches experience this magical barrier much earlier than others; that is, when they reach 750 in attendance, they experience the problems of the 1,000 barrier. Other churches go right past the 1,000 number up to 1,500 before they level off and can't grow. They experience the difficulties of the 1,000 barrier after they pass it.

The Megachurch Barrier

So, it's not the exact number that is the barrier, but certain factors within the large church make it difficult to break this barrier and keep growing. Growing a church is sometimes like growing children. Some boys reach their physical maximum strength at age 17; other boys do not reach their maximum strength until their late twenties. However, statistics show that the average boy reaches his optimum strength at approximately twenty-three years of age. I have arbitrarily set the barrier at 1,000, even though we are not sure that is the exact statistical point. Most church leaders can relate to a barrier of 1,000. Obviously, before your attendance reaches 1,000 you are dealing with a 3-digit number; after the church reaches 1,000, you are dealing with a 4-digit number. But these are superficial observations, and we come to the deeper question—Why is becoming a megachurch so difficult?

Some churches have hit the 1,000 barrier and kept right on going. Sometimes the pastor got "lucky," meaning the pastor's leadership had an unlimited vision, that is, a strategy without limitations and an ability to work their plan. But many churches were not "lucky"; they were stalled at the 1,000 barrier.

Unlimited strategy leads to unlimited growth.

What some observers described as "luck" was not really a lucky break in circumstances. Usually, the answer to growing churches resides in leadership. Some leaders had an unlimited vision that drove them to develop an unlimited strategy, which in turn produced sacrificial work by the followers and unlimited growth in the church.

1. *Uncharted waters.* Any navigator will tell you that it is dangerous to travel in uncharted waters. You don't know where the dangers are. You don't know when a crisis will hit or when you

will encounter a problem. Furthermore, you usually don't know how to solve a barrier, where to get help, or the long-range consequences of the problem.

In my early days of working with megachurches, many pastors hit a *space barrier* and could not grow past 1,000 because they didn't have room for additional worshipers. Most thought the only answer was to build a larger sanctuary. Today the answer may be multiple services. In the past, leaders were fearful of multiple services for two main reasons, which are reflected in the following quotations: "Two worship services will divide our church" and "I won't know everyone when we have two worship services." However, with time, many churches have conquered the *space barrier* by adding more than two services, and some have even added more services. Some churches have added different styles of services; others have added worship services on different days of the week.

2. *Growth itself becomes the barrier.* As the church gets larger, it becomes more complex simply because more people, more programs, and more options are present. Consequently, more problems arise. When you multiply the individual problems with organizational problems, the difficulty of producing growth increases exponentially. As a result, if a church can't solve the problems of its people in a middle-sized church, it cannot grow to the megachurch size. It becomes weighed down with a vast number of people who have unsolved problems or unsatisfied expectations. Like a boat that has gathered barnacles and moss, it moves slowly through the water. Some of the problems the pastor will face when he gets to 1,000:

• Increased number of personal problems among individuals.
• Increased number of paid ministers to manage.
• Increased number of paid staff to supervise.
• Building a cohesive vision to an enlarged following.
• Developing harmony among paid ministers and staff.
• Lack of parking.
• Inadequate size of the building.

- Logistical problems, that is, moving a larger number of people in and out of limited space in a short period of time.
- Need for increased finances to pay for expansion.
- Need for expert money management.
- Need for personnel administrators.
- Increased audio/sound problems.
- Worshipers are detached from platform in large auditoriums.
- Impersonalization among worshipers and between members grows.
- Senior pastor's inability to manage growing numbers of paid ministers and staff.
- Senior pastor's inability to delegate ministry through staff.
- Need for new forms of advertising to reach the masses.
- Unreached number of prospects in community dries up.
- The sin of an "Achan" is more likely to occur in a large ministerial or paid staff that will siphon off growth momentum and/or harmony.
- Burnout in senior pastor.
- As facilities grow older, institutional blight develops in buildings, organization, and/or vision.

3. *Lack of cohesion in the critical mass.* Every group of people has a critical mass and/or some type homogeneity that holds it together. I have often called this the glue that holds the individuals of a church together. Obviously, in the small single-cell church, the glue is physical family relationships or personal bonds between members. When you observe the multicell church, people still know one another in the small cells with which they identify, but another glue is added to the dynamic: the corporate vision the leader gives for growth or for the church's reason for existence. Then, when you observe the even larger multicongregational church, that is, the church of 1,000 or more, new problems kick in. As the congregation grows beyond 1,000, new people are added to the critical mass, but they are not bonded to a small cell within the church. They have not become a member of a prayer group or a

Sunday School class or they are not ministering anywhere within the church. They are just attending the church. By attending without bonding, the critical mass grows without any "glue" to keep the church members in a cohesive mass. They are just a crowd, not a true New Testament church body. Individuals no longer feel they are a part of the church family or a church group; they are simply individuals who attend the service, like those who buy a ticket to the theater. The only benefit they receive is from what is up on the screen or what's coming from the pulpit (see next problem).

4. *Platform growth without personal bonding.* Large churches grow on the strength of their platform. People attend a large church because of the attraction of the sermon, special music, personalities, praise band and/or orchestra, drama, the worship/liturgy, identification with a specific presenter, or any other platform attraction. One of the implied principles of the large church is:

The platform attracts but small groups bond.

When a church hits 1,000, it usually gives attention to increased quality in platform productions, that is, an outstanding Christmas pageant that includes drama, live animals, and flying angels, or other attractions that might be seen in a secular presentation. The church over 1,000 usually offers several special events each church year that attract visitors and potential members. As the attractions become more and more professional, the crowd becomes less and less cohesive, and sometimes the crowd becomes less and less bonded to the message of the church as presented through the pulpit. Therefore, platform growth through the 1,000 barrier may be the limitation that keeps a church from going beyond 1,000. In the Law of Diminishing Returns, the attractive methods a church uses to break the 1,000 barrier become the seeds of destruction that keep people from "bonding" to the church as it passes this barrier.

Obviously, the solution to this problem is small group relationships. Therefore, as the group approaches the 1,000 barrier, it must give attention to adult Sunday School classes, small-group cells, pastoral care groups, and/or recruiting people into service groups throughout the church ministry.

Relationships are the glue
that bonds people to a church.

5. *Space limitation.* As the church grows larger, it must accommodate its growing population with additional seating. Usually a church builds its first auditorium with approximately 175 seats. Some build larger, some build smaller; but most auditoriums are constructed to accommodate a single-cell family church. The second auditorium is roughly twice the size; it can seat approximately 400 worshipers. When a church fills its 400-seat auditorium, the middle-sized church often has the flexibility and leadership to continue growing through multiple services. Most churches cannot grow beyond two or three multiple services. Therefore they must build a third auditorium, which usually can seat approximately 1,000 worshipers. Even in an auditorium that seats 1,000 worshipers, intimacy between the participants and the pastor on the platform can be preserved.

But how big is too big? Some church auditoriums become so large, they become counterproductive. For example, an auditorium is too large when the worshiper cannot identify with the pastor who is preaching or the singer who is leading in worship. The configuration of the pews may determine the intimacy of the people one with another, as well as help worshipers identify with the platform. Sometimes a lower ceiling makes people feel closer to one another, whereas an auditorium of 3,000 or 4,000 seats with a very tall ceiling lacks intimacy. It may have the "feel" of a civic center or an arena, and the vast space separates people and isolates them from the platform.

I have preached in many churches of 1,000, and I have preached in several churches that will hold approximately 10,000. I preached in the Jotabache Church of Santiago, Chile, with 17,000 present (approximately one city block on the ground floor). I have also preached in the Full Gospel Church, Yoido, Seoul, South Korea. According to Pastor Yonggi Cho, this church will seat 25,000 people. For denominational meetings, I've preached in movie theaters, civic arenas, and in football stadiums. At what point does the crowd get so large that individual worshipers lose identification with the pastor and/or musicians on the platform?

In my experience, when an auditorium has more than 7,000 in attendance, something is lost in identification between the worshiper and the pastor. One pastor said to me, "You can't identify with people if you can't see the whites of their eyes." He continued by saying that when people are beyond the peripheral edge, they have more difficulty identifying with the heart of the sermon.

Delivering a sermon is not the same as reading a speech. In a sermon there is reciprocity between the minister's heart and the heart of those who are listening. As the minister pours his heart out into the hearts of the people, they should respond with like passion and pour their hearts out in return. However, there comes a time when the distance between the pew and the pulpit makes reciprocity impossible. If the worshiper cannot see the physical eyes of the pastor, it may be difficult to feel passion with their hearts. Then too, as the audience gets larger, those on the peripheral edge who are not identifying with the pastor, allow distractions to bother them. Those who are not listening because of distance and lack of intimacy begin moving and whispering; hence they bother others.

Obviously, some on the peripheral edge will pay attention whether they are sitting in a 2,500-seat auditorium, a 100,000-seat Olympic stadium, or listening by radio or television in another location. Their deep need becomes the catalyst for bonding with what the minister is saying. Therefore, personal need can over-come the barriers of space and distractions.

Another factor needs to be considered in regard to the size of the worship space. Some pastors communicate well because of their body language. But those same pastors cannot communicate when people can't see or perceive their body language. Some communicate well to listeners they can see but cannot communi-cate well over the radio or through a loudspeaker system. There-fore, to keep on growing, some pastors not only need to give attention to communicating by body language; they must also give attention to delivering a message by written script so they can communicate to those beyond their sight.

6. *Changes in leadership style.*[2] A church of 100 in attendance needs a pastor who will minister to the needs of the people of that church. His primary role is ministering leadership. When a con-gregation becomes a middle-sized church of approximately 400, the pastor must possess managing leadership skills. The pastor does not do all the ministering; he has many ministers who work with him. Therefore, the pastor must manage the ministers and their ministry to get the maximum contribution from each. When the church reaches 1,000, the pastor's leadership skills must again change. In the large church the pastor will exercise executive lead-ership. The executive leader gives attention to two areas. First, the executive pastor evaluates the past to learn from it, so the church can overcome its weaknesses and/or problems. Therefore, by executive leadership, the pastor must know his church well and be able to direct surveys, research, and receive reports from all areas of the ministry to evaluate the past in order to make plans for the future. Second, the executive pastor must attend to the future vision of the church. In dealing with the future, the executive pas-tor must know trends, the potential of the church, and his own potential; and then cast the dreams and/or vision. The second task of the executive pastor is carried out by visionary leadership.

The executive pastor does not manage the ministers in the large church. Rather, he delegates this responsibility to someone. For a large church to continue growing beyond 1,000, the executive pastor must employ a staff coordinator/leader to whom all of the ministers in the church answer.

Therefore, in order to break the 1,000 barrier, the pastor must be willing to give up ministry in certain areas and delegate it to ministers assigned to that area. The executive leadership pastor must also be willing to give up the coordination of other pastors, if not all pastors. The executive leadership pastor must learn how to influence a large staff of people and the even larger congregation of people. Like the captain of an aircraft carrier, the captain does not steer the ship; a sailor on the wheel is responsible to do that. The captain of an aircraft carrier has many workers who answer to him and supply him with information. They include the officers in charge of weather information, personnel, defense, fighter pilots and planes, as well as a medical officer. The captain of an aircraft carrier leads a crew of over 3,000 people by one way and one way only—decision-making. In order to be able to make decisions, he must have accurate information, he must know his equipment, personnel, and the potential of what his aircraft can do, and he must know the enemy. Therefore, the captain is a decision-making leader. In the same way, the pastor of a megachurch leads by decision-making.

7. *Limited pastoral leadership.* The greatest ability of the senior pastor is his leadership ability. Leadership involves attracting, recruiting, training, motivating, and giving a vision to those who follow the senior pastor. Therefore, the major source of growth in a large church is the pastoral staff that gathers around the senior pastor. Because the senior pastor will not be able to minister to all the people, he must attract leaders who can minister to all people. Therefore, to attract a quality staff, the senior pastor must possess the following qualities:

a. *Ability to discern spiritual gifts, temperament, and past experiences.* Some senior pastors are unable to pastor a large church simply because they cannot gather a competent staff around them. Some senior pastors are so compassionate that when they choose staff members their compassion hinders them from making good choices. They do not see potential staff members for what they are; a compassionate pastor sees potential staff for what he wants them to be or how he thinks he can help them grow into a new staff position. As a result, his inability to choose a staff member keeps him from becoming a growing pastor of a growing church. It is not the senior pastor's lack of preaching ability, lack of ministering to people, or his lack of spirituality that prevent him from pastoring a growing church effectively; the barrier to growth may simply be his inability to choose adequate ministers to minister with him.

b. *Ability to train staff ministers.* Sometimes a senior pastor is so committed to ministering to the flock that he does not give time to minister to his staff, equip his staff, or direct his staff. The senior pastor mistakenly thinks his staff is as motivated or as smart as he is. However, if his staff members were as motivated or as smart as he is, they might have a church as large as his. Therefore, a mistaken assumption by the senior pastor keeps his church from growing. A senior pastor must understand that his staff members need training, direction, motivation, and accountability. Therefore, the senior pastor must devote time to his staff or hire a competent coordinator who will equip them for ministry.

For the pastor to climb the ladder of effectiveness in building a superchurch, he must realize that many staff members will hold the ladder for him to climb. The secret is delegation; the senior pastor must delegate ministry to staff members so they can climb together to pass 1,000.

c. *Ability to find leaders who can minister.* Sometimes the senior pastor will look primarily for spiritual people when looking for staff members. His desire to employ staff members who are godly will blind him to the need to recruit staff members who are also efficient leaders. On the other extreme, some pastors only get efficient leaders who are able to work within the system, but they sacrifice spirituality.

The first step to finding staff members is to remember the words of Jesus: "Then Jesus went about all the cities and villages, teaching in their synagogues, preaching the gospel of the kingdom, and healing every sickness and every disease among the people. But when He saw the multitudes, He was moved with compassion for them, because they were weary and scattered, like sheep having no shepherd. Then He said to His disciples, 'The harvest truly is plentiful, but the laborers are few. Therefore pray the Lord of the harvest to send out laborers into His harvest' " (Matt. 9:35–38 NKJV).

The recruitment example of Jesus is a four-step process. First, Jesus saw the needs of people as he ministered to the multitudes. Second, he was moved with compassion to help people. Third, he gave a vision or challenge to his workers that the harvest was plentiful. The fourth principle of Jesus was, "Pray for the Lord of the harvest to provide workers." Therefore, the senior pastor must pray for spiritual workers and trained workers. Notice the emphasis on workers; they must be willing workers who work.

d.   *Ability to attract workers.* A basic principle in leadership is that *a leader attracts what he is, not what he wants.* Some pastors know that attendance will grow if they have soul-winners on their staff or in their congregation; therefore they preach soul-winning or try to attract people who are soul-winners to their staff. But people who are soul-winners are not attracted to those who are not soul-winners. A pastor attracts what he is, not what he needs. This is a natural principle of leadership, but even this natural law can be modified by the pastor who is a visionary leader. The pastor can cast the vision for soul-winning, and when that vision is a realistic goal of the church, the senior pastor will be able to attract soul-winners to his staff. Therefore, even when the senior pastor is not a great soul-winner, if he understands the need for soul-winning from the New Testament and includes that as one of the primary aims of the church, his burden for soul-winning will attract soul-winners. It's not what the pastor does that attracts a soul-winner; it's the pastor's burden that attracts. Then the principle is applied. The senior pastor's burden will attract ministers to work with him.

8. *Projection of needs onto the congregation.* If the pastor offers the wrong type of ministry to the congregation, the church will not grow. To put it in marketing terminology, the people are not buying what the pastor is selling. As an illustration, some churches grow large because the pastor is a Bible-expositional preacher. Every Sunday morning he teaches the Word of God, and people are attracted to the church because they want their pastor to be a Bible-teaching pastor. However, many who visit the church do not stay or even return. They come looking for a heart experience on Sunday morning, but they get their intellects filled by logical Bible teaching. Since people's emotions are not stirred, they do not come back to the church. After a period of time in the community, many people have visited the church expecting their emotions to be stirred only to leave with their expectations unfulfilled. Therefore, the pastor cannot reach a group of people in the community because he has limited his ministry to people who want Bible knowledge.

For a church to pass the 1,000 barrier, the senior pastor must continually look to the diversity of needs within his community and realize that he cannot meet all the needs. Therefore, he will allow the singles' pastor to have a ministry to singles; perhaps the singles' pastor will even offer a church service that focuses on meeting the needs of singles. The singles' pastor may preach differently from the senior pastor or may offer a different style of worship. When a senior pastor cannot share the pulpit or a worship service with a singles' pastor, that church has excluded itself from outreach to the singles. Therefore, to have unlimited growth among singles, the church must have an unlimited vision on reaching singles and an unlimited strategy that will attract singles. The same can be said of high school students, young marrieds, and those who want their emotions stirred. If your music bent is only to quiet contemplation, those people who need excitement and stirring each Sunday will not come to your church.

The church must offer diverse platforms to attract a diversity of people. These should include:

- The teaching of Bible exposition, so that people will learn and be stretched intellectually.

- Opportunities to ask questions, so that people will have their questions answered.

- Time for evangelism, when the Gospel is presented from the pulpit so that the lost are confronted with Jesus Christ and given an opportunity to respond to him and be converted.

- Meditative liturgical services, so that people will have the opportunity to be still and know that the Lord is God (see Ps. 46:10).

- Times to shout praises to God with excited hearts that bubble with enthusiasm.

Those pastors who take a church past the 1,000 barrier must be characterized by leadership, that is, *executive leadership*. Those who pastor the small church, are usually characterized by ministry. Those who pastor middle-sized churches break the 400 barrier because they are characterized as managers, that is, they manage those who minister to people.

To Take Away

We are so close to the emergence of multiple megachurches in America that we haven't had time to evaluate their long-term success. We know that in the short term they reach more people, they are on the cutting edge of innovation in ministry, they reflect boomers, and they reflect technology. But what do they do to people over the long haul? We know that a small church is a family church and that in a small church many children take over their parents' pew and their parents' place of leadership. But will the large church keep families from generation to generation? We know there is stability in small churches, but will large churches be that stable? Will large churches produce ministerial candidates? Will large churches be more likely to slip into heresy, or will they be the defenders of the faith? Will sin more easily creep into the total body of Christ through large churches than through small ones? We don't know the complete answers to these questions because those large churches haven't been around long enough for us to know the answers. However, we do know that barriers to becoming a large church exist and that large churches do have unique problems.

Benefits of Being Large

The large church has benefits that should be emphasized.[3] First, the large church is scriptural (Acts 2:41; 4:4; 5:14; 6:7). Second, the large church can saturate a large area by evangelism (Acts 5:28; 19:10). Third, the large church has more members, hence a larger diversity of spiritual gifts to minister to more needs and give a larger sphere of ministry (1 Cor. 7:7; Rom. 12:4–8). Fourth, the results of preaching the gospel to all (Mark 12:15), making disciples of all, and baptizing, then teaching them all things (Matt. 28:19–20), results in a great harvest, that is, a growing church. The Great Commission implies a large church. Fifth, fruit is the result of growth. The Bible teaches that all growing things will reproduce themselves (Gen. 1:12, 28–29). The large church is the result of growth and fruitbearing. Sixth, a large church can influence the social, political, and economic life of a large area for good (Acts 19:11–41).

In conclusion, many barriers are present to prevent a church from reaching the 1,000 level, and the large church with over 1,000 attenders has some unique problems. But like those who fought and won World War II, it is worth the battle. The war brought many losses, heartaches, and difficult times, but the battle was worth it for those who fought, for their families, and for their children's children. If they hadn't won World War II, then what? If we don't build large churches, then what? Will Christianity be stronger or weaker? The option is not left to us but to God. He is the Commander in Chief; we simply follow orders and do his will to bring him glory.

CHAPTER EIGHT

Adding Cells and
Congregations
to Break 1,000

I had an appointment with David Yonggi Cho, pastor of Yoido Full Gospel Church, Seoul, Korea, in June 1978 (at the time his church averaged 170,000 in attendance; today it averages over 600,000).[1] Cho met me at the door to his office and said, "Before I give you this interview, I want you to write that we are the largest church in the world, because the baptism of the Holy Spirit gives us power in evangelism."

Cho indicated that he had read all of my writings and that I tended to be consumed by Sunday School statistics and American laws of church growth. He did not want people to think his church was the largest in the world because of laws or statistics. Cho felt that many Americans were rationalistic, and they attributed all the growth of their churches to programs, rules, and techniques. He said to me, "Americans think by principles, but Asians think by metaphors and similes."

Cho then reminded me that the Bible writers were Asian, and that they used pictures in the Bible to portray church growth. They did not necessarily use laws. Then Cho asked me, "What picture of the church in the Bible is most often used?"

I answered him, "The body . . . the church is most often likened to a body."

Cho agreed with me, and then he asked me where the body came from. I knew he didn't want an answer, so I allowed him to explain. He held two fingers almost together, not quite touching. Then he said to me, "The body begins as a cell, so small it cannot be seen with the naked eye. The first cell of the body can only be seen with a microscope." Cho explained that when the semen of the man joins the egg of the woman, together they form a small cell. Then he announced, "Everything that the body is going to become when it is full grown is seen in that first cell."

At this point Cho began joking with me. He said that if we could see the first cell that formed his body, we would see a beautiful, olive-skinned oriental man with lots of black hair. Then he said, if we could have seen your first cell, we would have seen pale, white skin and a bald-headed man. We laughed, and from that moment on, we became close friends.

Cho explained to me that the body does not grow by growing a cell. As a matter of fact, he said to me, when a cell grows it is called cancer. When a cell grows it is diseased and leads to sickness or death. But then he gave me in a single embryonic sentence the key to growing a church.

"The body grows by the division of cells."

He said the first cell in the body divides to become two cells. Each cell is identical, and an observer cannot tell which one was the original cell. Even if we examined the cells as they divided under the microscope, we would see two identical cells coming from the first cell. Then we would see four, eight, sixteen, thirty-two, sixty-four, etc.

Local churches grow by adding new cells. New cells can be additional Sunday School classes, home Bible studies, service cells such as ushers, prayer cells, support cells, or even task-oriented cells such as committees, commissions, and boards.

Cho told me in 1978 that he planned to have 500,000 worshipers in attendance every Sunday. He said that if he did it the American way, that is, by building auditoriums, Sunday School classes, fellowship halls, etc., he could never reach that goal. He said that in 1978 he ministered to 170,000 people weekly in approximately 17,000 cell groups all over the city. Furthermore, Cho said, "If we built Sunday School rooms for the cells, we'd have a church campus as large as UCLA campus in Greater Los Angeles, California." He mentioned that the university's campus spanned approximately 150 city blocks.

"We don't have the money to build 17,000 classrooms, and the city officials wouldn't let us do it."

Cho used living rooms in homes, recreational rooms in apartments, offices, and restaurants. (I saw one cell meeting in a Burger King near the hotel and asked to join it for the evening.) A vital part to large church growth is, "The church body grows by the addition of new cells to which its people belong."

The Single-Cell Church

To understand the large church, one must understand the small cells that make up the large church, that is the single cell and the single-cell church. Therefore we revisit the small single-cell church to understand the different components of large churches (see chapters 1, 2, and 3).

A small single-cell church probably has an average attendance of 87 worshipers (87 is a statistical average of a wide variety of churches representing different denominations, theological convictions, worship styles, and regional areas of the United States). The single-cell church resembles a large, overgrown family. As a matter of fact, the single-cell church is often called the family church or the typical American church.

The typical single-cell church has five blood family or marital family groups; these family groups are the dominant influences of the single-cell church. The single-cell church is described by the following paragraph:

In a single-cell church everyone knows everyone, everyone relates to everyone, and everyone waits on everyone before anyone will do anything.

The above definition of a single-cell church in actuality is a definition of the homogeneous unit.[2] The sameness, relatedness, and dependency present in the homogeneous unit are also descriptive characteristics of the single cell. The pastor of a single-cell church is employed to minister to the congregation, not to be a leader of the church. As previously mentioned, the primary influence and/or control in the single-cell church is with the five families, and they usually are the board members or they influence the board.

Because "the body grows by the division of cells," new cells must be added for the single-cell church to grow. Usually these few cells do not come from within, but must come from the pastor and/or by the initiative of some outside force. The following initiatives by the pastor are workable tools to move the single-cell church past 100, so that it becomes a middle-sized church. When these things happen, the single-cell church begins growing toward 200 worshipers or even 300 worshipers.

HOW TO BREAK A SINGLE-CELL CHURCH AND GROW

1. Add an additional service.

2. Add additional Sunday School classes that are not age graded or gender graded, so that they can grow beyond their age or gender restrictions.

3. Begin specialized ministries (singles, special needs, bus, etc. These become a new cell/center of growth).

4. Hire a functional specialist (such as a youth pastor, who will create a strong, new youth cell that will produce growth). The more specialists hired, the greater the potential for growth.

5. Move into an enlarged building (usually organization and programs fill the available space, so that an additional building will usually create new cells within the church).

Just as the human body grows by the division of cells (and remains healthy by the addition of cells), in the same way the local church body will grow by adding cells. Don't think of adding people to a church of 100—think of adding new ministries, new classes, and new programs of outreach.

The process of growth involves a simple sequence:

1. See a new need;

2. Share a new vision;

3. Recruit new workers;

4. Train and share the vision with new workers;

5. Begin a new ministry and/or programs by new workers; and

6. Correlate new ministries with existing ones.

Just as fruit on trees and bushes grows on new sprouts, so growth in an existing church comes through new units, not through old units, classes, or groups.

	Different Names
1	The small church
2	The single-cell church
3	The family church
4	A homogeneous church
5	A class Sunday school church
6	A neighborhood church

The Middle-Sized Church

The middle-sized church is not always described by numbers, but rather by its constitution and/or the way it is organized (see chapters 4 and 5). When a church has several cells, it becomes a middle-sized church in its composition. A middle-sized church might have several elective Sunday School classes, some of which produce competition that causes growth. At the same time, some classes will not grow. As the classes begin to grow, traditional members are heard to complain, "I don't know everyone in the church," and "We are becoming two churches." These two criticisms are actually a sign of health; they indicate that the church is growing toward becoming a middle-sized church.

The primary role of the pastor in the middle-sized church is to be *managing leader*, that is, the pastor manages several people who do ministry in the church. The pastor should be shepherd to all the people, but when a youth pastor is hired, the pastor delegates his ministry to the youth pastor and extends his pastoral ministry to the young people through the youth pastor. The same

	How to Grow a Middle-Sized Church
1	Develop the pastor into a managing leader.
2	Add additional worship services.
3	Allow youth or singles to develop new worship services.
4	Carefully recruit ministry specialists who can grow ministries.
5	Prepare congregation for innovation and change.
6	Give attention to assimilation and bonding of new members into a cell.
7	Find new ways to market the various ministries to new publics.
3	Expand the organization and add new programs.
9	Add additional Sunday Schools.
10	Offer excellence in music, sermons, platform, and sound system.

process is repeated with a children's pastor, a singles' pastor, perhaps a music minister, and maybe later, a minister of recreation. As the church becomes more specialized, a middle-school pastor, a young adult pastor, and even a senior saints' pastor are added. When all of these additional pastors/ministers are added to the church staff, one of the major tasks of the senior pastor is to manage and/or organize his pastoral team for more efficient ministry throughout the church. Management becomes a key force in the middle-sized church very quickly, so the pastor must quickly develop skills as a managing leader.

Some pastors who preach well in single-cell churches are called to middle-sized churches. Sometimes they fail, however, because they cannot manage well or their organizational skills are counterproductive. These pastors fail in middle-sized churches not because of their pulpit ability, but due to their lack of leadership ability.

Someone has said that, in the small church, the pastor is the ball carrier on the football team. In the middle-sized church, the pastor is the quarterback who hands off the ball to a ball carrier. The pastor doesn't do all the ministry; he delegates it to staff members who in turn do ministry.

	Different Names
1	The middle-sized church
2	The multicelled church
3	The departmentally graded Sunday school church
4	A heterogeneous body with homogeneous cells

The Large Church

The most dominant force that produces growth in a large church is the pastoral leader, previously called the *executive leader*. In earlier writings, I said that the pastors of megachurches were the length and shadow of the church. By this I meant that because they were men of great ability and great character, they produced a great church.

A large church is actually a congregation of congregations, and within the congregations are cells. One third of the cells are probably related by blood or marriage.

A cohesiveness among the congregations and/or cells is usually present. Sometimes the cohesiveness or glue is nationality, neighborhood background, similar needs, similar desires, work relationships, family relationships, or some other designated glue that holds the group together.

The large church usually thinks of itself as "one big happy family," but in fact, it is anything but a big, happy family. When a large church is not growing, its leaders often think that if they can make things simpler and smaller, they can get it back growing again and/or they can reach out to the neighborhood. Again, the opposite is true; they must recognize the complexity of the large church for what it is, and the desire to be simpler and smaller may kill outreach rather than take it to a new level.

People who don't understand the large church think it is a small church with a lot of people. That's not true. Decision making in the small church is usually made in a business meeting by majority vote. As the church becomes middle-sized, more and more decision-making moves to the pastoral staff and/or the church leaders. When the church arrives at the megachurch status, decision-making passes from the congregation to small cells within the church. These small cells can include the pastoral staff, the finance committee, mission committee, advertising committee, or any committee that oversees a ministry within a large church. Neither the people of the group nor the larger congregation make decisions, the supervisory cell and/or board does. Sometimes it seems that the larger the church the longer decisions are in process. It has been said that in the large church "decisions are not made, they happen." This means that decisions are not made easily, like at a small-church business meeting. Decision making is more complex because many people are involved in the process of arriving at every decision.

The pastor is the *executive leader* who must coordinate the decisions of the congregation. Rather than being the person who makes the decisions, he must know who the decision makers are and where various decisions are made within the church; and he must make sure that the right decisions are made at the right place by the right person. In this role, the pastor becomes a coordinator of decisions, not always the one who makes decisions.

How to Grow A Large Church

1	The pastor moves up to an executive leader and a person is appointed as managing leader. The ministerial staff is accountable to the managing leader as he is accountable to the senior pastor.

2	The pastor must be a growing leader and maturing Christian statesman, because large churches are built on the pastor's longevity.
3	Pastor gives priority to vision (the future) and evaluates (the past).
4	System to monitor attendance and bonding.
5	Multiple educational systems, not just Sunday school.
6	Multiple worship services of various worship styles.
7	Schedule events to attract visitors and guests.
8	Give attention to attendance and assimilation.
9	Continue growth through new programs and ministries.
10	Give attention to buildings, parking, and user-friendly facilities.

The following diagrams represent the four kinds of churches and illustrate one possible structure for each.[3]

The "Xs" in the single-cell church represent the members. Because of the size of the illustration, the 8 "Xs" are symbolic of a whole church, not an exact number. A single-cell church has an average of 87 members. The smaller circles located inside the multicelled church and multicongregational church are fellowship circles that represent the primary groups or cells. A cell may be a choir, Bible study group, a Sunday School class, or a service organization.

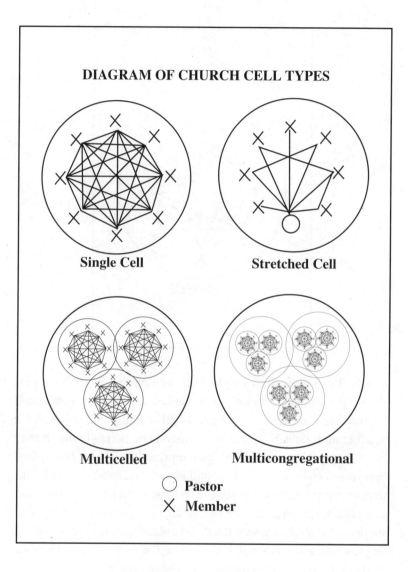

DIAGRAM OF CHURCH CELL TYPES

Single Cell

Stretched Cell

Multicelled

Multicongregational

○ Pastor
✕ Member

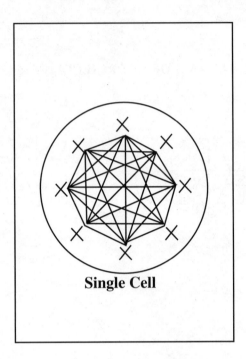

Single Cell

The illustration shows eight "Xs" in a circle. Each "X" represents a person, but obviously a single-cell church has more than 8 people. This illustration is symbolic of a single cell. Actually, a small church does not have just 8 members; a small church may have 40 or 87 people. The lines represent the relationships of everyone to one another in a small church. Remember the definition: everyone knows everyone, everyone relates to everyone, and everyone waits on everyone before anyone will do anything. The single-cell church is interrelated and cohesive. It is hard to grow a single-cell church beyond 100 because the members do not want to break the warm, interrelated fellowship they enjoy.

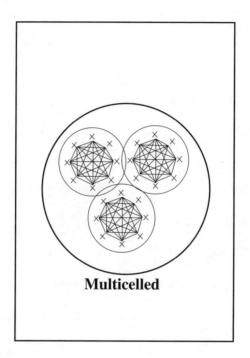

Multicelled

The middle-sized church is usually made up of three to eight single cells. These cells are about the size of a small church. They may include the youth cell, music cell, and the pastor's worship cell. New cells grow as the church adds ministers and new ministries. The middle-sized church becomes a multicelled church. The church in this illustration has only three cells, but it could have more cells.

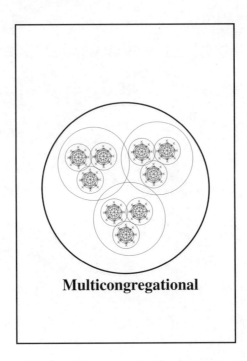

Multicongregational

The large church is not simply the total number of people who attend its services. The large church has a number of congregations. These congregations may meet at separate times or on separate campuses and may have separate ministers who lead each one. Sometimes all the congregations meet at the same time in the same auditorium and have the same ministers leading them. At these times this church is not designated by different roles, memberships, or seating assignments in the auditorium. Each congregation has its own "glue" that bonds the heart of each congregation to one another. One congregation may be comprised of the original members of the church, and the individual cells that make up that congregation are their kids, teens, and friends. A second congregation may consist of newcomers from around the church, new urbans with a different value system. Their values are the glue that holds them together. They know one another by their clothes, cars, restaurants, and sport choices.

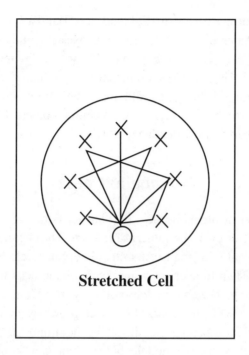

Stretched Cell

The larger a church grows, the more congregations and cells are needed to keep everyone bonded to their own center of identification. It truly is a heterogeneous body of homogeneous cells.

This drawing represents a unique situation in that the pastor is the focus of the members. The pastor in this church keeps the church going by ministry and leadership. Whereas the pastors in middle-sized and large churches give up their ministry to all by delegating it to staff ministers, in the stretch-cell, this pastor keeps ministering to all. This pastor is usually extremely gifted in ministry, and the church grows according to the limits of his ability. But this pastor is also gifted in leadership; therefore, some churches grow past 1,000 in attendance, but the members are attached to the pastor and his ministry, not necessarily to a small group with reciprocal fellowship.

The stretched-cell church resembles a "crowd," although it has some characteristics of a church, that is, a local church body. Lee

Roberson, former pastor of Highland Park Baptist Church, Chattanooga, Tennessee, said, "Everything rises and falls on leadership."[4] He was correct, but many heard the statement and misapplied it. They acted as if it meant, "Everything rises and falls on the pastor." When they did that, they built stretched-cell churches. A stretched-cell church is a church body of 100 that has a lot more than that in attendance.

Bonding to Cells[5]

The secret of breaking the 1,000 barrier is not advertisement, pulpiteering, or even the musical program. The secret is to bond each individual to a small cell so that everyone feels loyalty and dedication. Then to keep growing, keep adding cells to the large or megachurch. The church does not grow by adding individuals; that is only growing a crowd. The church grows by adding cells to which individuals belong. It's difficult if not impossible for a person to "bond" with 1,000 people, but a person can "bond" with 10 people in a Sunday School class or home cell.

The old term is to "join" a church, or to be "assimilated" into a church fellowship. These terms were adequate when the average American was loyal to the institutions of his community. The new term is *bonding*. When a person is bonded to a contemporary church, it is similar to the process of Super Glue. The old glue was paste or mucilage that just stuck two things together. In the same way, in the old days church membership was the adhesive that held the member to the church. This membership was usually determined by the common beliefs and behaviors of its constituency.

Super Glue is not an adhesive. It is a material that bonds two elements together, actually absorbing them into each other. The two fuse or melt into one. Paste will break and things that were pasted together will separate, even as people can disassociate from a local church.

Three steps are needed to bond a person to a church. The first step is *interfacing*. During this step the person must recognize the church, relate to the church where there are points of communication, and make an initial contact with the church. The second step is *buying into the church*. It is similar to a person walking into a store and buying an item or purchasing services. Buying includes need, desire, knowledge, and paying the price. It implies transference from the seller to the purchaser. An actual transfer of permission and authority takes place. When someone buys into a church, he not only has permission to be a member, he has authority to be a member with all the rights and privileges of membership. The third step in bonding is *ownership*. The person no longer feels it is the pastor's church. It is now his church. When a new member buys into a church and assumes ownership, he also assumes both responsibility and accountability. He is accountable to the new church, but he is also accountable to God.

When a person bonds to a new church, he must assume ownership of excitement, ownership of worship functions, and ownership of doctrine. New members must feel they possess the "contagious enthusiasm" of the new congregation and, to get it, they buy into the worship style. Notice that doctrine is the third item on the ownership list. On a priority scale, Americans generally feel it is not as important to buy into doctrine as it is to buy into "feelings" and "commitment."

We often feel that those who have been in the church for a long time are the real owners of a church; they are the first-class citizens. Those who later join are second-class citizens because they do not have a history of what is going on. However, in the church of the future, bonding into a church is knowing, feeling, and acting on the ownership of the church.

The word *bonding* means more than trying to keep a new member from dropping out of a new church. New members are best bonded to a new church when they belong to a primary group of the church. A primary group can be a Sunday School class, flock, cell, the ushers, a woman's missionary group, or the choir. A new member will identify with a primary group, which is a small group, rather than the total church or the larger group that worships on Sunday morning. The phrase "primary group" refers to the group with which a person identifies. The new member may not see himself as a member of the large congregation or megachurch, but he sees himself as a member of a small group. He can buy into the small group. Bonding takes place when the new member feels the small group can't adequately function without him because he is part of the process. "Those ushers need me," a new member says as he considers not attending church. When the new member projects himself into the small group, it becomes his "primary group" for identification with the church. A new member has bonded with the choir when she sings alto in the choir, sees herself as part of the worship process, and feels the process would diminish without her presence. She experiences church ownership with her small primary group, an experience that couldn't happen with the larger group.

Bonding is more than teaching prospective members habits of church attendance, getting their tithe, or correcting their behavior. Bonding is their total immersion into group fellowship, group values, and group ministry.

Bonding to the new group is often nonverbal and takes place without official instruction. This means that bonding does not automatically happen when a person goes through a new membership class or is voted into the church.

Bonding can begin taking place before the sinner receives Christ because it is part of the preconversion process. Bonding continues to take place after the act of receiving Christ and after the membership class is over because bonding is also involved in the postconversion process. Bonding is a process that is most effective when it occurs simultaneously with conversion.

Bonding is similar to the process of imprinting an act in the natural world whereby a newborn animal attaches itself through a sense of belonging to an agent that is responsive to it immediately after birth or hatching. A famous picture of the Nobel Prize winning naturalist Konrad Lorenz being followed by ducklings illustrates this point. The ducklings attached themselves to him as the protective parent. As with ducklings, bonding of humans produces relationships that can withstand separations. The ducklings followed Lorenz everywhere and did not unlearn the relationship during periods of separation. It is as though God has placed a divinely engineered factor, whether psychological or physiological, that prepares the newborn to become bonded to a parent.

Animals or fouls will identify with surrogate or substitute parents, especially if the real mother is absent or has rejected them. Apparently, the state of being "lost" and being "found," in a relational sense, contributes to bonding. Our contemporary world of anonymity and "lostness" prepares people for the bonding process of these new churches. At the same time, the contemporary world that does not understand loyalty and obligation does not respond to the normal classes on church membership.

To Take Away

The large church is more than a large crowd of people. It is made up of multiple congregations, and they in turn are composed of many small cells. Since people feel "one" with Christ in his heavenly body, they must feel "one" with him in the local body, and that includes feeling "one" with other believers. They, too, have Christ dwelling in their hearts, and they are united together in Christ.

While this chapter reflects some views of sociological bonding to the group and to each other, it is not grounded on social science. It is grounded on the Bible's teaching about the church. As you carefully study how each believer is united to one another, and to Christ in heaven, you will understand the necessity of bonding all believers to one another and all to Christ.

CHAPTER NINE

Leadership to Break
1,000

The one key ingredient to breaking the 1,000 barrier is the pastor-leader. The pastor must be an *executive leader* with skills not evident or required to break the two previous barriers.

To understand leadership, revisit J. Oswald Sanders who writes in his book, *Spiritual Leadership,* "Leadership is influence."[1] Therefore, when leading a megachurch, you must realize that the larger the attendance of a church, the greater the leadership skills needed by the pastor. More paid ministers and staff, more volunteer workers, more buildings, and more problems are present in a megachurch. Since leadership is influence, the pastor of a megachurch must give attention to the following: (1) how to influence, (2) what to influence, (3) where to influence, and (4) whom to influence.

In the book *The Eight Laws of Leadership*, a second description of leadership is given, "Leadership is plural."[2] The leader must take people with him on the journey. The pastor must relate to the people he is leading. Usually people will not follow someone they do not like and/or respect.

People look up to leaders.
Leaders look down to followers.

The processing of "looking" involves trust, respect, confidence, and commitment. When the pastor doesn't like his congregation (he may only be using it as a stepping-stone to a larger church), the healthy relationship that is needed to build a church is not present. Conversely, when the people don't like the pastor (they only tolerate him), the church is not growing healthier.

In describing pastoral leadership, the pastor is out front influencing parishioners. In the educational world, the teacher is out front influencing students, and in military circles the commander is out front influencing soldiers.

Leadership implies two things: movement and direction. A leader moves people toward a goal and gives them direction. Implied in this book is the goal of breaking the 1,000 barrier. The pastor must first lead the church to grow and then give direction through the 1,000 barrier. The following six laws of leadership will provide the pastor with some of the necessary tools to accomplish these objectives of movement and direction, and finally, breaking the 1,000 barrier.

The First Law of Leadership

This law, called "The Law of Vision/Dreams,"[3] is expressed in the slogan, "When followers buy into your vision, they buy into your leadership." Therefore, the secret of leading a church through the 1,000 barrier is for the pastor to set the vision or dream of a megachurch. This vision/dream must be more than numbers. It must be a vision of obeying the Great Commission, reaching people according to God's strategy, teaching people "all things Jesus gave," and maturing them in Jesus Christ, so that the church grows spiritually, grows healthy, grows in fellowship, grows financially, and finally, grows numerically. Then the church can break 1,000 in attendance.

The Second Law of Leadership

The second law of leadership is about rewards.[4] It says, "The leader gives rewards to his/her followers," because, "that which gets rewarded, gets done." Obviously, the rewards must be spiritual in nature. People must feel that their work and sacrifice are what Christ wants from them. There is little satisfaction for laypeople to break the 1,000 barrier for pride, numbers, bigger facilities, or more money. Perhaps this may be a motivation for the pastor and his reputation. Since secular people ask, "What's in it for me?" the people of the growing church will work and follow the pastor when they feel they are personally growing, their life is getting better, their worship is improving, and they are obeying Christ by bringing souls to him.

The Third Law of Leadership

The third law of leadership is credibility.[5] The followers must have confidence in their pastoral leadership to break 1,000, and the leader must be confident that his followers can follow, can achieve, and are worthy of his effort. The pastor-leader must have a credible plan and know how to implement it; the people must believe in their pastor and allow him to lead them.

The Fourth Law of Leadership

The fourth law of leadership is communication.[6] The pastor-leader must effectively communicate his plan so that the followers see the plan (understand), buy into the plan, desire to implement the plan, and will pay the price to make it happen.

John Maxwell points out an important difference between preaching and communication. While preaching deals with the content of the message, communication deals with the audience's understanding and acceptance of the message. Maxwell says that pastors who break the 1,000 barrier must go beyond preaching messages; the pastor must communicate a vision and plan to break 1,000.

The Fifth Law of Leadership

The fifth law of leadership is accountability.[7] People must be involved in the journey. If the pastor tries to take the journey past 1,000 alone, he'll never arrive at the destination. The pastor and the people must do it together. The law of accountability says in slogan, "Followers don't do what the leader expects (by vision or dream); they do what the leader inspects."

> Expecting must lead
> to inspecting.

This law of accountability implies building a good organization to involve everyone in the work of the church, so that the church ministers to everyone. Therefore, the pastor-leader must put administration in place that makes people feel accountable for taking the church past 1,000. In a crowd of 1,000, most individuals do not take responsibility for the crowd unless the leader builds an organization that makes them accountable. When the pastor-leader puts expectations on followers, the pastor is building a body. Every part of the body is interrelated to the other parts. The pastor-leaders begins with a vision of breaking 1,000; then the pastor-leader gets everyone involved.

> A pastor can't build a church *on* organization, but a pastor can't build a church *without* organization.

Remember, good organization and administration are not the purposes of ministry. They are a means to an end. The end goal is to glorify God, reach the lost, and build up believers.

The Sixth Law of Leadership

The sixth law of leadership is motivation.[8] The pastor-leader must give compelling reasons to reach the goal. Motivation is not appealing speeches, fancy talks, slick advertisement, or getting the followers excited. Church members follow a pastor-leader when they are given good reasons to work and sacrifice.

Great leaders motivate their followers to rise above average circumstances and sacrifice for the dream that has been communicated to them. They do more than simply tell their followers the dream. Leaders must know what people want and direct them toward it. Great leaders motivate their followers to rise above mediocrity, to overcome insurmountable obstacles, to make the most of limited resources, and to come out of difficult circumstances. Why? So they can achieve the dream.

The Strategy of Motivation

The effective pastor-leader knows how to move his or her followers to action.[9] Leaders must develop a strategy for motivation to grow and apply these laws to specific situations. Generally, the application of motivation strategy involves six steps.

1. You must know precisely what you are trying to accomplish. In this case the goal is to break 1,000. A goal is a dream with a deadline. Followers do not need a long speech or even a short speech from their pastor-leader to be motivated. They simply need to know where their leader is taking them— where they are going together. What kind of church will this be when we get there? In sports you must first know the goal of the game before you can score.

2. The pastor must know what response is needed from the congregation to reach the goal of 1,000 and what he wants his followers to do to reach the goal. The leader must be concerned about what to say to get the job done, possess a sense of conviction about what needs to be done, and be able to propose a series of action steps to help followers begin moving toward the goal.

3. A pastor-leader motivates by putting himself in the other person's shoes. To understand followers, the leader needs to be able to answer several questions.

What do they know? To motivate people, you must start where people are. Preachers are usually content centered. Communicators are usually listener centered. What they know about growth will color their perspective. If all a person has is a fork, everything looks like a meal. If all the pastor preaches is legalism, everything looks wrong.

What do they feel? Many people will emotionally respond to your leadership. If they are frustrated, they will respond in anger. They will not think with their heads. Most people respond from their hearts. Ralph Waldo Emerson illustrated this in a story about a farmer who tried to get a calf into a barn. A storm was coming that would endanger the safety of the animal, but when the farmer and his son tried to drag the calf into the barn, it resisted. When they tried to lift it, it was too heavy. Then the farmer's daughter appeared in the field and put her sugar-coated finger into the calf's mouth. As she continued dipping her finger in a pocket full of sugar and offering it to the calf, the calf willingly followed her into the barn.

What do they want? This question helps pastors identify expectations. Remember, "You can get everything you want in life if you help other people get what they want."

4. Expose and address major problems before followers raise them as barriers or obstacles. Successful pastor-leaders expose problems and answer them first, knowing that if their followers raise the problems, they will not move to the goal. They will give up or refuse to follow.

If you do not raise the problems first, some will think you are hiding something. Second, not dealing directly with the problem will color the issue in the thinking of followers. Third, existing problems will keep people from dealing with the sacrifice involved in reaching 1,000. The people will become problem oriented rather than goal oriented. Fourth, their problems tend to raise barriers and create negative feelings directed toward the pastor. Therefore, when leaders address the problems involved in reaching 1,000, especially the problems that everyone is aware of, followers gain confidence in their leadership.

5. Call for a commitment. Be prepared to ask people to sign on the bottom line. As a leader, be intentional because you will meet strong levels of resistance. Therefore, be prepared to win some votes and lose others. Successful leaders win more than they lose. They quickly forget about the losses, retaining only the lessons they learned.

6. Appeal to the higher vision of your followers. Those who are successful in marketing can see the higher dream. Maxwell states that people don't buy newspapers; they buy news. Women don't buy cold cream; they buy beauty. Teens don't buy records; they buy excitement. Church members won't

buy 1,000 as a goal; they want the spiritual results that come with reaching 1,000.

The Seventh and Eighth Laws of Leadership

The seventh law of leadership relates to problem-solving,[10] and the eighth law relates to decision making.[11] Obviously, a goal of 1,000 is a barrier or a problem. How can the pastor get or keep the church moving toward that goal? The pastor-leader's ability to solve problems and make decisions is an indication of the quality of his leadership and a predictor of his success to break 1,000 in attendance.

Pastor-leaders make good decisions on good information and bad decisions on bad information. Without any information, they make lucky decisions. Good luck means their decision worked; bad luck is usually blamed on others or the devil.

The bottom line in decision making is information gathering and processing. The success of a pastor-leader rests in his ability to know and remember the principles, data, solutions, and people that will help produce growth. What the pastor doesn't know, he must know where to locate. This involves knowing books, resources, programs, consultants, and organizations that can help the church break 1,000.

Five Steps in Decision Making[12]
Face the problem
Define the problem
Get as much information as possible
Choose a solution
Make the decision work

After studying the laws of leadership, a pastor must apply them to the unique problems of the megachurch and then apply them to his church in its unique setting. The following list of twelve principles will begin to help you solve barriers that hinder growth.

Twelve Principles Applied[13]

1. *Leadership gives direction of the organization.* When a church wants to grow past 1,000 in attendance, it must have an aggressive leader who gives movement and direction to the organization. Leadership involves four things: vision—the leader must have a vision of what the church will look like on the other side of 1,000; the path—the leader must know the way through the 1,000 barrier; the people's task—the leader must know what the followers will do to take a church past the 1,000 barrier, and what the church that grows past 1,000 will do for the followers.

2. *Leadership determines the timing of the organization.* Like most things in life, when a leader tries to move a church past 1,000, timing is imperative. A leader must know when to cast the dream, when to mobilize, when to make long-range plans, when to move, and, considering all of these factors, when not to move. Timing is everything in breaking barriers.

3. *Structure determines the size of the growth.* To move a church past 1,000, the pastor should not first think of going after the people, advertising, or doing any type of program to attract the people into the church.

The pastor must first enlarge the structure. There is an old adage that simply says, "Don't make the foot fit the shoe." That means you can't force a big foot into a small shoe, and you can't force a large number of people into a structure that is too small for them. The secret is to get big shoes for big feet or create a big structure for a large congregation.

Three people can make it possible for 100 or 1,000 viewers to see a movie at a theater: a ticket salesperson, an usher, and a projectionist. But in growing a church you are building a body. You must build a structure for a big body if you expect a big attendance.

Some pastors have tried to squeeze big feet into small structures. That's like having hurting feet and worn-out shoes. When you make the foot fit the size of the shoe, everything is wrong and nothing feels right. You cannot pour a liter of Coca-Cola into a six-ounce glass, nor can you pour a pot of coffee into a single cup. So you cannot put 1,000 into a church auditorium that seats only 500. And by the same rule, you cannot attract 1,000 to a church with an organizational structure for 100 people.

When thinking of moving toward the 1,000 barrier, you must grow your staff. That means you must have adequate managers, adequate administrators, and an adequate organization.

Second, you must grow your structure, which means you must have adequate committees, lines of management, and a total organization that will attract and keep 1,000 people.

Third, you must grow your budget. Even though you don't have the money, you must plan the budget for 1,000, then reach people to take you to 1,000, all the while paying for a program with less than 1,000. As asked over and over again, "What came first, the chicken or the egg?" so the pastor might ask, "What comes first, the people or the money?" In this sense, they both come together. You must attract both people and money to break the 1,000 barrier.

Recently a pastor who was trying to break the 1,000 barrier asked me, "Why haven't we grown?" This pastor was looking at casual things such as style of preaching, his visitation program, even the advertisement in the newspaper.

"You haven't structured your organization for growth," I told him.

Many preachers know how to set up extra chairs to grow, but they don't know how to start a second service. Some pastors can figure out a way to squeeze 550 or 600 people into a church with a seating capacity of 500. But to break the 1,000 barrier, they must come up with a new strategy. One suggestion might be to start a second service so that 1,000 people can be accommodated for worship on any given Sunday.

Years ago one young man was making more tackles than anyone else on a football team. He thought he would be number one in the draft, but to his surprise, all of the scouts overlooked him. Finally he went to a scout and said, "Why didn't you choose me?" He told him, "Your body structure tells me you are as big as you are going to be. Another player on the team will grow another 30 to 50 pounds in the next four years. We need somebody who is 50 pounds heavier than you to make our team." The scout went on to tell him that he was good enough for his present team, but he was not big enough to go to the next level.

Many pastors are good enough for the 500 level. At the same time their churches are as big as they are going to get, and their structures and buildings are as big as they are going to be. To go to the next level, that is, 1,000 in attendance, they have to "add 50 pounds."

4. *Those closest to the pastor will determine the size and growth of the church.* It is a fact of leadership that those closest to the leader will determine the quality and success of leadership. In the same sense, those closest to the pastor will determine the growth of the church. Therefore, the pastor must surround himself with people who can grow the church past the 1,000 barrier.

When John Maxwell first went to Skyline Wesleyan Church, Lemon Grove, California, attendance was averaging 1,000.[14] Maxwell looked at the pastors in the room and gave them the analogy of fleas in a jar. After someone put a pane of glass on top of the jar, the fleas continued to jump against the pane of glass but always fell back into the jar. Then the pane of glass was taken off, but the fleas never jumped higher than the top of the jar because they were conditioned after falling back into the jar over and over again. Maxwell went to the chalkboard and drew a line across the center of the chalkboard, then wrote 1,000 on the line. Above that he drew a second line and wrote 2,000. Then Maxwell said rather candidly, "I know everyone in this room can build a church of 1,000, because you have taken this church to 1,000."

Maxwell then explained that the church was going to the next level of 2,000. But he explained that none of them had the experience of taking a church past 1,000 because they had not worked in a church larger than that one. "I don't know if anyone here can go with us to the next level," he told them.

With that, Maxwell threw out a challenge for them to grow personally because he was going to grow personally. He challenged them to journey with him to 2,000.

Your pastoral staff is either your greatest asset or your greatest liability to break the 1,000 barrier. Everyone who begins the pastoral journey with the pastor in the church won't end the journey with him. If a church is going to grow, some of the present staff of the church may not be capable of growth and will have to leave.

5. *The relationship skills of the pastor create the spirit of the church that will determine if the people want to take the church past 1,000.* Part of becoming a great leader is relating to the people of the church. It has often been said,

A great leader has followers who
believe in him,
because a great leader first
believes in them.

Growing a great church is built on the pastor relating to his people. I have said, "Leadership is plural." By that I mean that the pastor must know his people, love his people, be willing to sacrifice for them, and make them the focus of growth.

If the pastor takes the church
growth journey alone,
the pastor never arrives at the
destination.

You cannot use your people to grow a church to reach numbers. The church is people; the church is the body of Christ. And every member who has Christ is the church. So don't think in terms of 1,000 as a numerical goal, think in terms of 1,000 people as your goal. When you know 1,000 people and bond them into relationships with one another, then the church becomes many groups making up one single multitude. That church is preparing itself to move to another level.

6. *The prayer of a church determines its passion, and passion determines if it will break the 1,000 barrier.* To move a church past 1,000, the pastor must mobilize prayer partners. Prayer partners will pray for the pastor, the people, and the outreach of the church. They will also intercede for power in soul-winning and ask God to do miracles in breaking through barriers.

7. *Determine if breaking the 1,000 barrier is easy growth or expensive growth.* The phrase "easy growth" means that the church's sanctuary will seat 1,000 people. Perhaps it is an old church that used to have more members. If you have access to a large auditorium, you don't face an expensive building campaign. All you have to do is fill it. And if you have parking for 1,000, that is another plus. You don't have to worry about construction of an expensive parking lot. This is easy growth. You can make internal changes, expand the structure, institute new programs, share the vision, and begin outreach. You can move toward 1,000 the easy way.

But if your sanctuary will only seat 300 and your attendance is 500 meeting in two services, you face expensive growth. You have to add a third worship service and hire staff members, then expand the organization. You will have to add new ministries, new places of ministry, new ministers. But to expand the church beyond 1,000, you probably have to construct more buildings. The price of buildings gets more expensive every year. And the nicer the building you construct, the more expensive the price.

Growth stops when the price gets too high. Some pastors and boards have decided that the price of growth is too high. They don't want to hire the architect, build the facilities, and construct the parking lots. They have decided not to grow.

8. *The pastor must not need his people.* Obviously, a pastor needs people, just as a fish needs water. This word *need* means to depend upon people in the congregation to fulfill his ego on self-determined ministry. The most codependent person in the world tends to be the pastor. He depends upon his people to fulfill his ego, and he needs them as much as they need him. He knows that when they have problems, they will come and depend upon him. It is difficult for the pastor to delegate ministry to someone else and to walk away from ministering to people, because he needs them to fulfill his life. It is difficult for some pastors to create new programs and ministries that will meet the needs of the people when they are not present. Furthermore, some pastors find it difficult to allow ministry that they do not control to take place in their churches. If you are a codependent pastor, it will be very difficult to take your church beyond 1,000 in attendance.

9. *The pastor must be secure if he is going to lead a church past 1,000 in attendance.* Part of being a good leader is being secure in your spiritual gifts and calling from God. Insecure pastors have difficulty delegating ministry to others; they want to do it all. If a pastor is secure, he can bring a leadership team around him to grow the church past the 100 barrier or past the 1,000 barrier.

Pastors must be secure enough to allow someone else to preach to their people and to allow their people to depend upon someone else in the church. A senior pastor must be secure enough in his management skills to allow ministers that work for him to be just as successful as he is and to support all that he does. It is amazing what you can do for God if you don't care who gets the credit.

10. *Not everyone who begins the journey to 1,000 will end up at the destination.* A pastor must begin the journey into ministry with people who cannot go all the way with him. If a pastor is a "seven" (using a scale of one to ten) in leadership ability, he usually attracts parishioners and staff members who are "threes,"

"fives," and "sixes." It is against human nature for a pastor who is a "seven" to hire somebody who is a "nine" or a "ten."

The pastor who is a "seven" begins the journey by growing himself before he will grow his church. The pastor will deeply love people who are "threes" in ministry. He will play golf with them and go to conferences with them. He and his wife will go out for a meal with this couple. They may even take vacations together. But somewhere in life, the "seven" pastor moves into a new level of leadership and has to leave the "three." That person will stay in a smaller church or gravitate to a ministry where he feels comfortable.

Some ministers on the staff will help a pastor get the church to where it is at present, but some of those same staff members can't help get the church past 1,000. Therefore, difficult decisions await that pastor when he wants to move past the 1,000 barrier.

11. *Don't feel guilty when present staff members can't take the journey.* Usually those who can't take the journey to 1,000 don't want to take a trip beyond where they are now. They would be unhappy going past 1,000, and you are not doing them a favor by making them go where they are not equipped to go or do not feel comfortable going. And if you decide to stay where they are, you have violated your spiritual gifts. When you determine to stay in *their* comfort zone, you step out of God's will. What you say by staying with your friends is that you refuse to take the journey that God has put in front of you.

12. *Increase the number of influences in your church so it can grow past 1,000.* John Maxwell teaches the Pareto Principle, that is, 20 percent of the people are the influences in the church, while 80 percent of the people are followers. This principle says that 20 percent of the people give 80 percent of the money. Twenty percent of the people do 80 percent of the work, and 20 percent of the people carry 80 percent of the prayer burden.

In reverse, 20 percent of the people have most of the personal problems that demand church attention, 20 percent of the people take up 80 percent of the pastor's time, and 20 percent of the people cause 80 percent of the problems in the church.

Applying the Pareto Principle in business, look at your corner convenience store. Twenty percent of the products on the shelf produce 80 percent of the income. On the other hand, 80 percent of the products bring in only 20 percent of the income. Some people think they can cut back inventory on the 80 percent so they can stock up on the 20 percent of the inventory, and thus make more money. But then the percentage on the whole is restructured and you lose that percent of the profit that is equal to the loss of inventory.

To have 1,000 in attendance, you must have at least 200 influences. These are prayer members, board members, Sunday school teachers, and people who carry out ministry and bear the burden of finances. Therefore, to build a church past 1,000, give attention to training more people to be influences or spiritual movers and shakers.

A good exercise to help you see the potential in your church is to make a list of the top ten influences in your church. Next, make a list of the top 20 percent of the influences in your church. From this list determine how many people you need to train to be influences so you can break the 1,000 barrier. Obviously, you need 200 influences to break the 1,000 barrier.

Good leadership structures the church around the influences. Bill Hybels talks about the "Point Man" principle. He says, "I do not begin ministries because there is a need, or because there is space, or for any other reason. I do not begin a ministry until I have a man or woman to walk *point*. This point person is the one who has the vision for the ministry; he sacrifices and pays the price, doing everything possible to get the ministry operational." This is another way of saying to organize your ministry around influences.

When you want to grow your church, look at people and always look to influence. Don't always begin with job descriptions. Sometimes when you look at job descriptions, you may bypass the person who is a strong influence, a leader. Don't overlook the leader who does not have the particular skills you need in a job. If that person is a strong influence in your church, reverse your strategy! Hire influences. They are the quality people who will learn the skills to do the job where you put them.

To Take Away

The pastor who would build a church must be *humble,* realizing that it is God who works through all of his abilities no matter how strong or lacking. He must have vision as the prophet of the Old Testament who was called a "seer" (1 Sam. 9:9) because he was the eyes for God—seeing first, seeing farthest, and seeing the most. The pastor who would break barriers in a church must, by faith, see the church completed in his heart before a soul is won or a brick is laid on the foundation.

Courage is another attribute of the church builder; he must face discouragement and disappointment. Some of those whom he leads to Christ will turn their backs on the Lord. Other young babes in Christ will not grow according to his expectations. No congregation will grow as rapidly as the pastor expects, nor will the new building be as elaborate as the pastor desires. He needs courage to accept the present without letting discouragement rob his future.

Compassion is another needed quality. Who can grow a church without the love of God flowing through him? The church-growth pastor must love people, want to be with them, and desire to serve them.

Tenacity is needed in every successful life. The pastor cannot build a megachurch without persevering; he must never give up. A church is an endless struggle. Because he senses God's call to a community, he does not turn back because of opposition. Since he has a burden from God for a city, he rejects calls to other pastorates. "[Jesus] steadfastly set his face to go to Jerusalem" (Luke 9:51 NKJV), where he would die for his people. The pastor must have the same determination. He will build a great church because he made a promise to God and to himself.

The church builder must embody all the qualities of the Christian life because, as the shepherd of the flock, he is the example. Being controlled by the Spirit in his preaching, teaching, soul-winning, and church management is only the first step. The church builder must display the fruit of the Spirit in his personal life so that others will desire to be like him. If the list of qualities for a church builder were complete, it would be as long as the New Testament requirements for any pastor. To make the qualifications short and understandable, he must simply be "God's man" in the community, doing what Christ would do.

This chapter has focused on the barriers or problems of breaking the 1,000 barrier. Some pastors have broken this barrier without even knowing that 1,000 was a barrier. To some, 1,000 is just a stepping-stone to the next level of growth.

John Wooten is universally recognized as one of the greatest basketball coaches of all time. Yet he didn't do what many latter-day successful coaches do. Wooten didn't scout his opponent. Wooten believed his greatest opponent was within himself and his team. He felt that if he could get his team members ready to play their game and follow their strategy, they could win.

Sometimes when we spend too much time on the opponent, it makes us pessimistic instead of believing. It makes us defensive instead of aggressive. It makes us react instead of act. If pastors place too much emphasis on the 1,000 barrier, they may forget the assets going for them. They may forget that "greater is he that is in you, than he that is in the world" (1 John 4:4 KJV). They may forget that "I can do all things through Christ who strengthens me" (Phil. 4:13 NKJV). They may forget, "Whatsoever ye shall ask in my name that will I do" (John 14:13 KJV).

EPILOGUE

All Growth Has
Upper Limits

The chief end of man, according to the Westminster Catechism is, "To glorify God and to enjoy Him forever." The chief end of your life is not to grow, but to obey God, serve God, and glorify God on your growth journey. Growth is not the goal; it only helps you reach that goal. The same goes with churches.

The chief end of churches is not to break the 100 barrier, the 400 barrier, or the 1,000 barrier. Your church may break these barriers on the journey, but numerical growth is not the destination of a church's journey; it's the by-product of carrying out the Great Commission and glorifying God. We are to take this journey because Jesus sends us as the Father sent him (John 20:21). We are to preach to everyone: "'Go into all the world and preach the gospel to every creature'" (Mark 16:15 NKJV). And what results should we expect? Jesus told us, "'Make disciples of all the nations, baptizing them in the name of the Father and of the Son and of the Holy Spirit, and teaching them to obey everything" (Matt. 28:19–20 NIV). We are to be Jesus' witnesses "in Jerusalem, and in all Judea and Samaria, and to the ends of the earth" (Acts 1:8 NIV).

When the church obeys Jesus, it will grow, even though Jesus did not command it to grow. He only expected growth when the right things were done. Paul described the destination of our growth journey: "To the measure of the stature of the fullness of Christ" (Eph. 4:13 NKJV). Being like Jesus is reached by growing: "May grow up in all things into Him who is the head—Christ" (Eph. 4:15 NKJV). So each believer in the body is to faithfully serve and obey, "Every part does its share, causes growth of the body for the edifying of itself in love" (Eph. 4:16 NKJV).

Nothing will continue to grow forever, because if it did, it would be limitless—only God is infinite, that is, without limits. The world is only so big, and we only have so much time till Jesus returns, so growth has upper limits. They are God's limits, not ours. No one has ever done all he can do, no church has reached all it can win to Christ, no human organization on earth is perfect. We can all do more, both individually and collectively in our churches. Let us press on to be like Jesus. Let us work diligently until we can work no more.

Our prayer for this book is that God will be glorified in the growth journey of each church and by the destination that each church reaches. Each church could probably have done more, but we look at what each church has accomplished. May God be glorified in what was done for him. May God be glorified—*panta ta ethne*—in all nations.

Endnotes

Introduction

1. C. Peter Wagner, *The Healthy Church* (Ventura: Regal Books, 1996).

Chapter One

1. Rick Warren, *The Purpose Driven Church* (Grand Rapids: Zondervan Publishing House, 1995), 16.

2. Lyle E. Schaller, *The Multiple Staff and the Larger Church* (Nashville: Abingdon Press, 1980), 28.

3. David A. Womack, *The Pyramid Principle of Church Growth* (Minneapolis: Bethany Fellowship, 1977), 82.

4. William C. Tinsley, *Upon This Rock* (Atlanta: Home Mission Board, 1985), 83.

5. Carl S. Dudley, *Making the Small Church Effective* (Nashville: Abingdon Press, 1978), 19.

6. Ibid., 34–35.

7. Schaller, 28.

8. Tinsley, 83.

9. Douglas A. Walrath, *Planning for Your Church* (Philadelphia: The Westminster Press, 1984), 24–26.

10. Lyle E. Schaller, *Tattered Trust* (Nashville: Abingdon Press, 1996), 129.

11. Dudley, 49.

12. Lyle E. Schaller, *The Small Church Is Different* (Nashville: Abingdon Press, 1982), 53–54.

13. Dudley, 53.

14. Lyle E. Schaller, *44 Ways to Increase Church Attendance* (Nashville: Abingdon Press, 1988), 14.

15. Dudley, 49.

16. Lyle E. Schaller, "Why Forty Is a Fellowship Barrier," *Leadership* (Fall 1984): 48.

17. Dale E. Jones and Richard Houseal, "Research & Trends," *GROW* (Spring 1996): 44.

18. Dudley, 49–50.

Chapter Two

1. Lyle E. Schaller, *The Small Church Is Different!* (Nashville: Abingdon Press, 1982), 45.

2. C. Peter Wagner, *Your Church Can Grow: Seven Vital Signs of a Healthy Church* (Ventura: Regal Books, 1976), 187.

3. J. Robert Clinton, *The Making of a Leader* (Colorado Springs: Navpress, 1988), 46.

4. Lyle E. Schaller, *Getting Things Done* (Nashville: Abingdon Press, 1986), 58–59.

Chapter Three

1. Jack W. Hayford, *Prayer Is Invading the Impossible* (New York: Ballantine Books, 1977, 1983), 53.

2. Paul [David] Yonggi Cho, *Successful Home Cell Groups* (Plainfield, N.J.: Logos International, 1981), 162.

3. C. Peter Wagner, *Leading Your Church to Growth* (Ventura: Regal Books, 1984), 79.

Chapter Four

1. Lyle E. Schaller, *The Middle Sized Church* (Nashville: Abingdon, 1985), 7.

2. Ibid.

3. Ibid.

4. See Thom S. Rainer, *Eating the Elephant* (Nashville: Broadman & Holman, 1994).

5. This study will be published in Thom S. Rainer, *High Expectations* (Nashville: Broadman & Holman, 1999).

6. C. Peter Wagner, *The Healthy Church* (Ventura: Regal, 1996), 135–48.

7. These two studies were published in Thom S. Rainer, *Effective Evangelistic Churches* (Nashville: Broadman & Holman, 1996) and *High Expectations* (see note 5).

8. Schaller, *The Middle Sized Church,* 109.

9. See Rainer, *High Expectations.*

10. From the study cited in note 5.

11. Ibid.

12. Dean Kelley, *Why Conservative Churches Are Growing.* Rev. ed. (Macon, Ga.: Mercer University, 1986).

13. See Rainer, *Effective Evangelistic Churches*, chapter 7.

14. See Rainer, *High Expectations.*

15. Ibid.

16. Rick Warren, *The Purpose Driven Church* (Grand Rapids: Zondervan, 1995).

17. See Rainer, *High-Expectation Churches.*

18. Wagner, chapter 2.

19. Ibid., see chapter 7.

20. Ibid., see chapter 8.

Chapter Five

1. The results of our studies have been published in Thom S. Rainer, *Effective Evangelistic Churches* (Nashville: Broadman & Holman, 1996) and Thom S. Rainer, *High-Expectation Churches* (Nashville: Broadman & Holman, 1999). In order to qualify as an "evangelistic church," the church had to have reached at least 26 people for Christ in the years studied (typically measured by baptisms), plus have a conversion ratio of less than 20:1 (The conversion ratio is: total resident membership divided by annual baptisms (or similar measure of conversions).

2. See Thom S. Rainer, *Eating the Elephant* (Nashville: Broadman & Holman, 1994), 184.

3. Rainer, *Effective Evangelistic Churches*, 67.

4. Ibid.

5. The definition used in the research project upon which the book *High-Expectation Churches* is based.

6. Rainer, *High Expectations.*

7. Ibid.

8. My first research of this nature was reported in Thom S. Rainer, *Giant Awakenings* (Nashville: Broadman & Holman, 1994).

9. Dean R. Hoge, Benton Johnson, and Donald Luidens, *Vanishing Boundaries* (Louisville: Westminster/John Knox, 1994), 200.

10. My use of the "dinosaur" metaphor comes from a book about Sunday School: Ken Hemphill, *Revitalizing the Sunday Morning Dinosaur* (Nashville: Broadman & Holman, 1996).

11. Unpublished data from the research which resulted in the book by Rainer, *High Expectation Churches.*

12. See my book on this leadership approach: Thom S. Rainer, *Eating the Elephant.*

13. From a conversation with author, October 1997.

14. Billy Graham, "Recovering the Primacy of Evangelism." *Christianity Today* (December 8, 1997), 29.

15. Ibid.

Chapter Six

1. Elmer Towns, *The Ten Largest Sunday Schools And What Makes Them Grow* (Grand Rapids: Baker Book House, 1969), 4.

2. Ibid.

3. Ibid., 11.

4. Elmer Towns, John Vaughan, and David J. Seifert, *The Complete Book of Church Growth* (Wheaton: Tyndale House Publishers, Inc., 1981), 341–67.

5. Elmer Towns, *Ten Innovative Churches* (Ventura: Regal Books, 1990), 204.

6. Jerry Falwell and Elmer Towns, *Church Aflame* (Nashville: Impact Books, 1971), 11–12.

7. Rick Warren, *The Purpose Driven Church* (Grand Rapids: Zondervan Publishing Co., 1995).

8. Towns, *Ten Innovative Churches,* 177–91.

9. Elmer Towns, *A Practical Encyclopedia of Evangelism and Church Growth* (Ventura: Regal Books, 1996), 78–79. This is the most complete statement of definitions, descriptions, and historical background on the Church Growth Movement.

10. Elmer Towns, *The Successful Sunday School and Teacher's Guidebook* (Carol Stream, Il.: Creation House, 1976), 198–213. The term *synergism* was first used in relationship to Sunday School growth, with application to church growth. I used the analogy of the dynamics of a shopping center as opposed to individual stores that were isolated from one another. I defined the phrase to mean explosive growth in a large Sunday School coming from many ministries that produces numerical results that were greater than the sum total of all ministries.

11. Towns, *Ten Innovative Churches,* 163–73, 237–45.

12. Carl George, *How to Break Growth Barriers* (Grand Rapids: Baker Book House, 1991).

Chapter Seven

1. Elmer Towns, *The Complete Book of Church Growth* (Wheaton: Tyndale House Publishers, Inc., 1981), 341–67.

2. George Barna, general editor, *Leaders on Leadership* (Ventura: Regal Books, 1997). This book by 14 authorities describes and defines the various roles of leadership.

3. Jerry Falwell and Elmer Towns, *The Church Aflame* (Nashville: Impact Books, 1971). This appears to be the first book to give the advantages of size to local churches.

Chapter Eight

1. Elmer Towns, John Vaughan, and David Seifert, *The Complete Book of Church Growth* (Wheaton: Tyndale House Publishers, Inc., 1981), 61. This chapter was perhaps the first to examine the causes for the growth of the Yoido Full Gospel Church, Seoul, Korea.

2. Elmer Towns, *A Practical Encyclopedia of Evangelism and Church Growth* (Ventura: Regal Books, 1996). See articles on "Homogeneous Unit" and "People Movement."

3. Elmer Towns, *FRANGELISM: A Network Program for Local Church Outreach* (Lynchburg, Va.: Church Growth Institute, 1985). This program was first copyrighted in this resource packet that local churches used to train its members to evangelize their FRAN's, i.e., their friends, relatives, associates, and neighbors. The term FRANGELISM means "to evangelize people through existing relationships."

4. Elmer Towns, *The Ten Largest Sunday Schools and What Makes Them Grow* (Grand Rapids: Baker Book House, 1969). See chapter 2. It describes the ministry of Dr. Lee Roberson who is credited with first coining the statement on leadership.

5. See the following for a full discussion of the topic of bonding people to a church body. Elmer Towns, *Ten Innovative Churches* (Ventura: Regal Books, 1990). See chapter 15, "New Bonding: From Joining a Church to Buying into a Relationship."

Chapter Nine

1. J. Oswald Sanders, *Spiritual Leadership* (Chicago: Moody Press, 1967), 19.

2. Elmer Towns, *The Eight Laws of Leadership* (Lynchburg, Va.: Church Growth Institute, 1992), 9–14.

3. Ibid., 21.

4. Ibid., 37.

5. Ibid., 47.

6. Ibid., 61.

7. Ibid., 71.

8. Ibid., 85.

9. Ibid., 89. The following outline is taken from this chapter.

10. Ibid., 97.

11. Ibid., 107.

12. Ibid., 111.

13. John Maxwell and I attended a conference of the megachurches that was associated with the Independent Church churches. This conference was held in Palm Springs, Calif., January 1997. The following outline comes from a discussion with this group. The majority of the ideas came from Maxwell, whom I credit with influencing my thinking on leadership.

14. Elmer Towns, *Ten Innovative Churches* (Ventura: Regal Books, 1990). Chapter 1 has a history of the growth of Skyline Church and a description of Maxwell's leadership.

Bibliography

The Small Church
C. Peter Wagner

This is the best current literature dealing explicitly with the small church. Some of the authors argue that the small church has value in itself and should not grow, some make no judgment on the matter, and some urge growth.

Brown, Carolyn C. *Developing Christian Education in the Smaller Church*. Nashville: Abingdon Press, 1982. A practical workbook providing program ideas for nurturing members of the small churches. Very helpful.

Carroll, Jackson W., ed. *Small Churches Are Beautiful*. New York: Harper and Row, 1977. Thirteen valuable contributions by leading mainline-oriented church leaders. Not growth-oriented, however.

Cho, Paul [David] Yonggi. *Successful Home Cell Groups*. Plainfield, N.J.: Logos International, 1981.

Clinton, J. Robert. *The Making of a Leader*. Colorado Springs: Navpress, 1988.

Crandall, Randall K. and L. Ray Sells. *There's New Life in the Small Congregation! Why It Happens and How*. Nashville:

Discipleship Resources, 1983. The authors believe that small churches can grow, and they make their point well.

Dudley, Carl S. *Making the Small Church Effective.* Nashville: Abingdon Press, 1978. A well-written apology for small churches and their integrity. Not growth-oriented.

Exman, Gary W. *Get Ready . . . Get Set . . . Grow.* Lima, Ohio: C.S.S. Publishing, 1987.

Fowler, Harry (self-published). *Breaking Barriers of New Church Growth.* This deals with the barriers of 35, 75, and 125 that the new church faces.

Grubbs, Bruce, ed. *Helping a Small Church Grow.* Convention Press, 1980. A spiral-bound collection of eleven essays written by Southern Baptist leaders. This is one small church book that focuses on growth and is well worthwhile.

Hunter, George G. III. "Helping the Small Church Grow," in *Church Growth Strategies That Work* by Donald McGavran and George G. Hunter III. Nashville: Abingdon Press, 1980.

Hunter, Kent R. *The Lord's Harvest and the Rural Church.* Kansas City, Mo.: Beacon Hill Press, 1994.

Madsen, Paul O. *The Small Church: Valid, Vital, Victorious.* Valley Forge, Penn.: Judson Press, 1975. A sound study on the situation and problems of the small church. Soft on possibilities for evangelism and growth.

Maner, Robert E. *Making the Small Church Grow.* Kansas City, Mo.: Beacon Hill, 1982. Maner is a Nazarene pastor who has served small churches and tells here what God has done to make them grow.

Mavis, W. Curry. *Advancing the Smaller Church.* Grand Rapids: Baker Book House, 1968. A good, growth-focused book designed to help the small church get on its feet and grow.

Ray, David R. *Small Churches Are the Right Size.* New York: Pilgrim, 1982. A well-thought-out analysis of the nature of the small church with many creative thoughts for ministry there. Among ministry areas outreach and growth are not high priorities.

Schaller, Lyle E. *44 Ways to Increase Church Attendance.* Nashville: Abingdon Press, 1988.

———. *Getting Things Done.* Nashville: Abingdon Press, 1986.

———. *Multiple Staff and the Larger Church.* Nashville: Abingdon Press, 1980.

———. *Tattered Trust.* Nashville: Abingdon Press, 1996.

———. *The Small Church Is Different.* Nashville: Abingdon Press, 1982. With characteristic insight and clarity, Schaller has authored probably the most helpful book on understanding small churches yet published. It is value free as to whether small churches should grow.

Sullivan, Bill. *Ten Steps to Breaking the 200 Barriers.* Kansas City, Mo.: Beacon Hill Press, 1988. This book gives general principles of growth but doesn't give analysis of barriers.

Tinsley, William C. "Looking at the Small Church: A Frame of Reference," *The Christian Ministry* (July 1977). For a short article, this has a wealth of insights on the dynamics of the small church.

———. *Upon This Rock.* Atlanta: Home Mission Board, 1985.

Wagner, C. Peter. *Leading Your Church to Growth.* Ventura: Regal Books, 1984.

———. *Your Church Can Grow: Seven Vital Signs of a Healthy Church.* Ventura: Regal Books, 1976.

Walrath, Douglas Alan, ed. *New Possibilities for Small Churches.* New York: Pilgrim, 1983. Several authors share valuable insights on the special ministry demands of the small church. Growth is not a priority in this book.

———. *Planning for Your Church.* Philadelphia: The Westminster Press, 1984.

Willimon, William H. and Robert L. Wilson. *Preaching and Worship in the Small Church.* Nashville: Abingdon Press, 1980. An excellent work focused on internal growth, not outreach and evangelism.

Womack, David A. *The Pyramid Principle of Church Growth.* Minneapolis: Bethany Fellowship, 1977.

Zunkel, C. Wayne. *Growing the Small Church: A Guide for Church Leaders.* David C. Cook, 1982. This is an extremely practical manual with extensive professional artwork for teaching the contents to others. It is much more than theory. If its principles are followed, the prognosis for growth in almost any small church will be good.

The Middle-Sized Church
Thom S. Rainer

Dudley, Carl S. *Making the Small Church Effective.* Nashville: Abingdon Press, 1978.

Hemphill, Ken. *Revitalizing the Sunday Morning Dinosaur.* Nashville: Broadman & Holman, 1996.

Hoge, Dean R., Benton Johnson, and Donald Luidens. *Vanishing Boundaries.* Louisville: Westminster/John Knox, 1994.

Rainer, Thom S. *Eating the Elephant.* Nashville: Broadman & Holman, 1994.

———. *Effective Evangelistic Churches.* Nashville: Broadman & Holman, 1996.

———. *Giant Awakenings.* Nashville: Broadman & Holman, 1994.

———. *High-Expectation Churches.* Nashville: Broadman & Holman, 1999.

Schaller, Lyle E. *The Middle-Sized Church.* Nashville: Abingdon Press, 1985.

Wagner, C. Peter. *The Healthy Church.* Ventura: Regal Books, 1996.

The Large Church
Elmer L. Towns

Anderson, Leith. *Dying for Change.* Minneapolis: Bethany, 1990.

Arn, Charles. *How to Start a New Service.* Grand Rapids: Baker Book House, 1997. Your church can reach new people by adding another worship service.

Barna, George. *The Frog in the Kettle.* Ventura: Regal Books, 1990. One of the great books on innovation that helped churches grow.

———. *The Power of Vision.* Ventura: Regal Books, 1992. A great book to find your vision, whereas most books by pastors of large churches tell the reader how to capture the pastor's vision.

———. *User Friendly Churches.* Ventura: Regal Books, 1991.

Chandler, Russell. *Racing Toward 2001: The Forces Shaping America's Religious Future.* Grand Rapids: Zondervan and Harper, 1992.

Galloway, Dale, and Kathi Mills. *The Small Group Book.* Grand Rapids: Baker Book House, 1995. The practical guide for nurturing Christians and building churches.

George, Carl. *How to Break Growth Barriers.* Grand Rapids: Baker Book House, 1991. This book called for pastors to break out of the shepherd mold and delegate authority. This book lacks (1) an analysis of why barriers exist, (2) practical steps to break barriers, and (3) the biblical basis for growth. This book emphasizes the metachurch concept; hence many who do not accept the "meta approach" will not learn many good lessons from this book.

George, Carl F., and Warren Bird. *Nine Keys to Effective Small Group Leadership.* Mansfield, Ohio: Kingdom Publishing, 1997. How leaders can establish dynamic and healthy cells, classes, or teams.

———. *The Coming Church Revolution.* Grand Rapids: Baker Book House, 1994. Empowering leaders for the future.

George, Carl. F., Warren Bird, and Ted Engstrom. *How to Break Growth Barriers*. Grand Rapids: Baker Book House, 1993. Capturing overlooked opportunities for church growth.

Martin, Glen, and Gary McIntosh. *Creating Community*. Nashville: Broadman & Holman, 1997. This book provides deeper fellowship through small-group ministry.

————. *Finding Them, Keeping Them*. Nashville: Broadman Press, 1992. Effective strategies for evangelism and assimilation in the local church.

Rainer, Thom, ed. *Evangelism in the Twenty-First Century*. Wheaton: Harold Shaw, 1989.

Schaller, Lyle E. *Assimilating New Members*. Nashville: Abingdon Press, 1978.

———— *The Multiple Staff and the Larger Church*. Nashville: Abingdon Press, 1980.

Schuller, Robert H. *Your Church Has Real Possibilities*. Ventura: Regal Books, 1975.

Spader, Dan, and Gary Mayes. *Growing a Healthy Church*. Chicago: Moody, 1991.

Towns, Elmer L. *A Practical Encyclopedia: Evangelism and Church Growth*. Ventura: Regal Books, 1995. This is the definitive statement of the Church Growth Movement stated in propositional forms. The articles are in encyclopedic format and arranged in alphabetical order.

————. *America's Fastest Growing Churches*. Nashville: Impact, 1972.

————. *Putting an End to Worship Wars*. Nashville: Broadman & Holman, 1997. Understanding: (1) why people disagree over worship, (2) the six basic worship styles, and (3) how to find the balance and make peace. While this book won't help a church grow, it will help the reader understand why there are six different ways to grow a worship service.

————. *The Ten Largest Sunday Schools and What Makes Them Grow*. Grand Rapids: Baker Book House, 1969. The first American church growth book.

————. *Ten of Today's Most Innovative Churches.* Ventura: Regal Books, 1990.

————. *Ten Sunday Schools That Dared to Change.* Ventura: Regal Books, 1993.

————. *World's Largest Sunday School.* Nashville: Thomas Nelson, 1974. A study of the Sunday School of First Baptist Church, Hammond, Indiana.

Vaughan, John N. *Absolutely Double!* Bolivar, Mo.: Megachurch Research Press, 1990. The story of miracles and explosive church growth at Sung Rak Baptist Church, Seoul, Korea, the world's largest Baptist church.

————. *The Large Church: A Twentieth Century Expression of the First Century Church.* Grand Rapids: Baker Book House, 1984.

————. *Megachurches & America's Cities: How Churches Grow.* Grand Rapids: Baker Book House, 1993.

Warren, Rick. *The Purpose Driven Church.* Grand Rapids: Zondervan Publishing House, 1995. Growth without compromising your message and mission.

Westing, Harold J. *Multiple Church Staff Handbook.* Grand Rapids: Kregel Publications, 1985.

Wimber, John, with Kevin Springer. *Power Evangelism.* San Francisco: Harper San Francisco, 1986.

Index